MW00644255

Chief Optimization Officer
Shattering the Status Quo

Scott Burgmeyer

&

Tammy K Rogers

Copyright © 2021-2022 by

Scott Burgmeyer & Tammera K Rogers

Published by: Happy Jack Editing and Publishing

Illustrations & Cover Design by:

Courtney Lampman

All rights reserved. No part of this publication
may be reproduced, stored in a retrieval system,
or transmitted in any form without prior written
permission of the publisher. The only exception is
brief quotations in printed reviews.

This book is a summary of research and
experience. Any resemblance to actual persons,
living or dead, or events are coincidental.

ISBN: 978-1-944104-37-5

DEDICATION

The book is dedicated to those who fall in love with the optimization journey.

TABLE OF CONTENTS

ACKNOWLEDGMENTS

Beth, Josh, Ben, Michael – thanks for your love and understanding as we worked on these concepts. Spending time away from you to create this has allowed us to share our learning with others.

Tony – thanks for talking with us at dinner in the summer of 2019 to spark integrating "Optimization" into our business.

To our clients and partners – thanks for allowing us in your organizations – it is (and will continue to be) great to see us all become more together.

Introduction

CHIEF OPTIMIZATION OFFICER
Shattering the Status Quo

The C-Suite of a typical multi-level company is comprised of individuals with varying talents, generally referenced with an array of alphabet-soup acronyms.

- The Chief Executive Officer (CEO) is the face of the organization and is responsible for the vision and direction of the organization, and ultimately – the company's success or failure.

- The Chief Financial Officer (CFO) takes care of the money.

- The Chief Operating Officer (COO) makes sure the day-to-day operations runs smoothly and product gets out the door on a timely basis.

- The Chief Human Resources Officer (CHRO) is in the people and culture business.

- The Chief Information/Technology Officer (CIO/CTO) manages the organization's technology.

- The Chief Marketing Officer (CMO) takes care of branding, marketing, and public relations.

So, what does a Chief Optimization Officer (COptO) do? They ensure the organization doesn't get stuck in the status quo.

> "They ensure the organization doesn't get stuck in the status quo."

COptO's push the organization to be more and do more than they have ever done before. They eliminate organizational complacency. They ensure that the organization remains competitive by enabling the company AND the people that work there – to level up, day after day, month after month, year after year.

Here's why we need a Chief Optimization Officer.

Individuals in the C-Suite are typically specialists. They bring a tremendous amount of expertise to the table. Each of them is responsible for a specific area of risk and/or opportunity, and they tend to see the world through very different lenses. When the C-Suite is brought together as a whole, their diverse perspectives allow them to view information, opportunities, and risks from different angles – enabling the organization to make better and more well-rounded decisions.

In our experience, most C-Suite organizational charts do not take advantage of a critical perspective... optimization.

We have specialists that:
- Protect and leverage our financial assets.
- Guarantee that we will deliver quality products or services on time.
- Ensure we have the right talent.
- Guard our data and exploit technology.
- Share our message and products so that consumers choose us.

What is missing is the specialist that is responsible for optimization.

op·ti·mi·za·tion (aap·tuh·muh·zay·shn)

We define optimization as a set of purposeful actions that makes the best or most effective use of a situation/resource to deliver outstanding results.

So, imagine for a moment what it would be like to have someone at an executive level whose primary responsibility is to figure out how the organization can BE more and DO more with the resources that the organization has RIGHT NOW. All without creating chaos.

"BE more and DO more with the resources that the organization has RIGHT NOW. All without creating chaos."

Optimization is not:
- Change management.
- Creating a ripple effect.
- Process improvement.
- Quality management.
- Employee engagement.
- Doing more with less.

Optimization requires:
- Simplicity.
- Measurement.
- Bringing People Along.
- Optimization Bursts.
- Incremental Growth.
- Facilitation Skills.

And it results in an organization that:
- Continually levels up.
- Rises to any challenge and remains agile and resilient.
- Has, keeps, and attracts the best talent.
- Constantly blows by the competition.

Now before you make a logic leap — and say something like:
- "Isn't that Quality's responsibility?"
- "Don't we have someone who does Lean or Six Sigma?"
- "HR can handle that — it sounds like Change Management."
- "That's Operation's job!"

Yes, you may have roles like this in your organization. AND...

Most organizations have a set point. A place where they comfortably get work done. It's the place and pace that the organization has become accustomed to. It is easy. And it is the status quo.

Changing the organization's set point, raising the bar, leveling up — that's NOT easy. And it's uncomfortable. The system, the people, and the organization itself are fighting to remain the same. And in THAT moment, the way the organization does things seems VERY appealing. But just like Bob Iger,

Disney's former CEO said, "The riskiest thing [an organization] can do is maintain the status quo."

Consider what happened to the retail giant, Sears, Roebuck and Co.

Tammy grew up in Chicagoland where the Sears Tower is a prominent feature of the cityscape. Sears stores played a memorable role in Tammy's childhood. Her family went to Sears for school clothes, work tools, kitchen appliances and auto repair work. They got their tetherball there. Every Christmas the kids would go through the catalogue and fold over the corners of the pages that had pictures of the toys they wanted. Sears was an institution.

Fast forward to 2021. What once was an anchor store at hundreds of malls across the country has been reduced to 34 retail stores nationwide. Was Sears simply a victim of the 2020 pandemic? No. As early as 1984, Sears was holding on dearly to their way of retailing while a new generation of discount retailers like Walmart and Target started to redefine the category.

Maintaining the status quo killed Sears.

Let's look at another example. In 1984 Tammy was working for a company called National Computer Systems (NCS). She traveled a lot, so her boss bought her a Compaq Portable computer. We're not sure why they called it  portable. Think luggable. It weighed 28 pounds!

At the time, the Compaq Portable was considered to be top-of-the-line.[1] In fact, Compaq set industry records with this model three years in a row (from 1983 to 1985) when they sold $111M, $328M, and $509M respectively.

So business was great...until Michael Dell came along. Dell chose a direct-to-user model that eliminated distributors and value-added-resellers which made Dell computers more economical. How did Compaq respond? They didn't. Compaq embraced the status quo. With all their earlier success, they believed they could sell their way out of the problem without changing their pricing or their product.

Compaq was sold to Hewlett Packard, at a discount, in 2001.

These stories are all too common. What once was a flourishing restaurant chain, retailer, manufacturer, tech giant, hospital, design house, engineering firm, association, or consulting company becomes a shell of itself – or disappears all together – because they were unable or unwilling to shed the status quo and adapt.

A COptO's responsibility is to eat the organization's status quo for breakfast.   Not just when big, systematic, changes are happening in the industry – it's eating the status quo on a DAILY basis.

"A Chief Optimization Officer's responsibility is to eat the organization's status quo for breakfast.

Baking optimization into the fabric of the organization provides long-term protection. It enables organizations to make small changes that lead to big results, such as saving thousands of overtime hours. It builds the resilience needed to see an organization through the tough times. It skills-up the organization for "do-it-or-die" challenges. And it normalizes the idea of becoming more.

This responsibility is simply too important to be left to chance. It's too critical to delegate. And it's too essential to expect one of the other C-Suite specialists to add it to their already-full plate.

We've been blessed to work with hundreds of organizations over the last 25+ years. And that time has been well spent. Working in the trenches alongside our clients has challenged us, pushed us, taught us, and humbled us. Without those experiences – we wouldn't be who we are today. And we wouldn't be writing this book.

The COptO role was a spark of an idea more than 14 years ago. One of our clients was struggling with legacy systems, processes, and rituals – all of which were being exaggerated by confirmation bias in the C-Suite. We couldn't fault the executive team. All of them were doing their jobs and, as we discussed the root cause, we came to realize that there was not a single person in the organization that was responsible for optimization. Eureka!

That was the first time we recommended a COptO role.

Since then, we've seen this opportunity and recommended this solution to a variety of clients. Some organizations found the idea to be too radical.

They didn't know of any other organizations that had this role, so they were unwilling to give it a try. Some had us support them in this role as an external set of eyes. Some organizations said yes, but only at a mid-manager level. A few organizations embraced the concept and added another specialist to the C-Suite.

If you know anything about Creative Solutions Group and Aveea Partners, the organizations that we lead, we tend to have long-term relationships with our clients. So, we've kept in touch with most of the organizations where we have made this recommendation. We still talk with the leaders in these C-Suites and they share their data with us. We've been fortunate enough to be able to measure their progress over time. And many of them will see their stories unfold in the following pages.

Sometimes these stories are flattering. Sometimes they are not. We ALL learn from both good and bad experiences.

We won't share the real names of the companies and people that made this book possible. We're grateful that we had the opportunity to learn together, and that we're able to share these learning lessons with you in the following pages.

So, if you're thinking that this new role sounds interesting, read on! We'll dig into what a successful

COptO looks like, and you'll discover some of the methodologies that a COptO can use to maximize the organization's return on investment.

If you're skeptical about the value of the role, read on. We will outline how organizations have used this role and share the hard results they achieved.

And, finally, if you're convinced that you want to be or need to hire a COptO, read on. We've written the world's first COptO job description!

PART I

THE
CHIEF OPTIMIZATION OFFICER
MANIFESTO

1

Awareness

"Your visions will become clear only when you can look into your own heart.
Who looks outside, dreams; who looks inside, awakes."
— C.G. Jung

An organization cannot grow beyond its leaders. Therefore, the organization's leaders are also the organization's governors. And just like an engine governor, it's the leader's actions and attitudes that determine the speed at which the organization can function. That is why awareness is so important in the Chief Optimization role.

"An organization cannot grow beyond its leaders."

Self-Awareness

Leaders who are self-aware are regarded as more trustworthy.[2] They have superior influencing skills.[3] Subordinates and their superiors consider them to be more effective than their non-self-aware counterparts.[4] And self-aware leaders increase organizational commitment.[5]

And that, ladies and gentlemen, is the fuel that allows an organization to put the pedal to the metal!

According to a study by Tasha Eurick, the author of Insight: The Power of Self-Awareness in a Self-Deluded World,[6] self-awareness is made up of two types of knowledge: Knowing who you are internally and knowing how other people see you.

And before you pat yourself on the back, here is the scary statistic. Eurick found that:
- 95% of people believe that they are self-aware
- But only 10-15% of people are actually self-aware

Wow! 85-90% of the population do not see themselves clearly and/or do not recognize how other people perceive them! Let that sink in for a moment. That means there is a very good chance that YOU and I are in that non-self-aware category. Ouch!

Let's paint a picture of what happens when companies hire someone who lacks self-awareness to drive change and continuous improvement throughout the organization...

Meet Paul.

Paul has the right pedigree. He went to the right kind of school to get his engineering degree and then went on to another prestigious school to get his master's degree in systems engineering. He spent his first two years of employment working for a small organization where he was the "process improvement guy." He identified the improvement opportunities. He collected and analyzed the data. He recommended and implemented the solution. And then Paul left that organization with a lot of data that proved that he had done good work and moved on to a large insurance company where he joined the Quality Team.

For the next seven years, Paul was assigned to lead Six Sigma projects where he identified problems, collected, and analyzed data, and recommended and implemented solutions – exactly what he had done at his previous company. It was during this tenure that Paul extended his education. He received his Six Sigma Black Belt and became an ASQ Certified Quality Engineer.

But Paul was frustrated in this job. He would say things like:
- "People" don't understand my role.
- "They" are afraid of change.
- "Leadership" talks a good game, but "they" don't support process improvement.
- "This organization" doesn't have any "discipline or accountability."
- [Other] people are "stupid" and "don't get it."

Paul's annual reviews were good, but he never received a real promotion. He always had that nagging feeling that something wasn't quite right. And he could not understand why people would not listen to him. He knew his solutions were good. The data proved that he was right. And yet – project after project – his perfect answers were not sustained long-term. So, when it became clear that he was not going to be promoted, Paul took his data and joined another company, this time as the Vice President of Process Improvement.

This was Paul's dream job. He knew that the CEO believed in continuous improvement. The organization had elevated the position so that it was sitting in the executive suite. And they were giving Paul the staff and latitude he needed to design and implement an organization-wide process improvement system.

And it was the perfect...storm.

Let's see how Paul's story unfolds as we walk through the Awareness Quotient (AQ).

Self-Awareness is Only the Beginning

Self-Awareness is the ante' that is required to be in the game. It's the baseline skill. And if a COptO really wants to succeed, he/she needs a set of skills that build on top of Self-Awareness.

"Self-Awareness is the ante'
that is required to be in the
game."

In addition to Self-Awareness, Chief Optimization Officers also need:
- Self-Management
- Social Awareness
- Stakeholder Awareness
- Organizational Impact Awareness

When you put all these skills together, you have the Awareness Quotient.

The Awareness Quotient

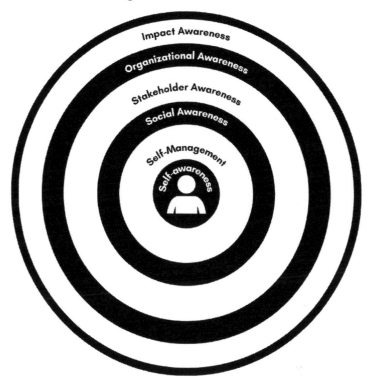

Self-Management

In his book, The Emotionally Intelligent Workplace, Daniel Goldman defines self-management as "the ability to regulate distressing affects like anxiety and anger and to inhibit emotional impulsivity."[7] In plain English, what he is saying is that individuals who self-manage don't let their emotions get the best of them. It is not that they don't HAVE or FEEL emotions – they do. Everyone gets angry, hurt, frustrated, ticked off, anxiety-filled, and downright pissed. Individuals who self-manage however, can experience those emotions and keep themselves from reacting or worse yet, over-reacting. They make conscious and intentional choices. They choose to RESPOND instead of jumping immediately into the fray.

Sometimes they choose to listen and consider another perspective. Sometimes they get curious and ask more questions. Sometimes they decide to de-escalate the situation. Sometimes they choose to wait for a better time. And sometimes they determine that now is the right time to have a difficult conversation.

Please do not misinterpret self-management as a method of conflict avoidance.

Self-management is not about choosing to avoid conflict. People who master self-management CHOOSE their next best step. They CHOOSE to act in a way that achieves the necessary end result. And they know that getting different perspectives and opinions on the table often leads to disagreement and conflict.

Researchers Drigas and Papoutsi say it this way: "With self-management, you become more flexible, more extroverted, and receptive, and at the same time less critical of situations and less reactionary to people's attitudes."[8]

Great self-managers know how to voice their opinions, listen to other points of view, disagree, fight for results, and land on a great solution – all without whispering behind other people's backs, creating an "us versus them" coalition, feeding into office politics, or attacking and "injuring" others. Self-management masters choose both WORDS and ACTIONS that invite thought and consideration. And, they don't settle for watered down, everyone-will-agree-with vanilla answers. They are willing and able to work through their emotions in a way that benefits the organization's bottom line as well as everyone who is involved.

> "Self-management is not about choosing to avoid conflict. People who master self-regulation CHOOSE their next best step."

Social Awareness

We define Social Awareness as the ability to recognize, understand, and successfully respond to the emotions of the people around you. And just like Self-Awareness is the predecessor to Self-Management,

Self-Management is the predecessor to Social Awareness.

If we look back at Paul's experience, we can see that he lacked Social Awareness. If you remember:

> *Paul's annual reviews were good, but he never received a real promotion. He always had the nagging feeling that something wasn't quite right. And he could not understand why people would not listen to him. His solutions were good. The data proved that he was right. And yet – project after project – his perfect answers were not sustained long-term.*

Look at all the social clues:
- He wasn't promoted.
- His gut told him something was wrong.
- People didn't listen to him.
- The data was good.
- The solutions were sound.

Here is the kicker. If the technical side of the equation is sound, then logically you are left with two options: It's either you or them.

And if you remember, Paul used some interesting language to describe his frustrations:
- "People" don't understand my role.
- "They" are afraid of change.

- "Leadership" talks a good game, but "they" don't support process improvement.
- "This organization" doesn't have any "discipline or accountability."
- [Other] people are – "stupid" and "don't get it."

Unfortunately, when Paul transitioned to his new vice president role – his frustrations went with him. You'll notice that Paul never once thought about how HE contributed to the situation.

Paul did not recognize that HE was at the heart of all the issues in his jobs. He saw himself as the guru – the person with all the answers, the "process improvement guy," and the knight in shining armor whose job was to ride in with the data and the right answers to save the day. Paul did not recognize that the people he was trying to save DIDN'T THINK they needed to be saved. Nor did Paul recognize that it was HIS job to get people pumped up and excited about the process improvement journey.

Paul, just like the research suggests, dug himself a bigger hole when he took on the Vice President title. Relative to lower-level leaders, managers with big titles and responsibilities significantly overvalue their skills and abilities.

And as an individual's organizational power grows, the research shows that a leader's self-awareness, social awareness, empathy, and trustworthiness skill gaps become even more pronounced.[9]

Where is Paul today?

At the same organization, with the same title, the same issues, AND,

- The organization has become change resistant.
- When Paul asks the C-Suite to support him, he gets head nods – but little else.
- Paul uses power and authority to get things done.
- The Process Improvement department has built a rigid system of checks and balances to ensure compliance with Paul's system.
- The Process Improvement team has put a lot of effort into lagging indicators – catching people doing it wrong and stepping in to "help" fix the issues.

Paul is not a bad guy. He is an AVERAGE guy.

And average players do not have social awareness. They are inside their own heads. They often believe that the measure of success is hard work, or a good solution, or the best product. And they spend so much time on THESE parameters that they forget that work solutions and products are dependent on other people.

Even the most extraordinary efforts of one person are often dependent on others. One individual usually cannot do it on their own. Other people must contribute. Other people must cooperate. Other people ultimately have to say yes. And wouldn't it be nice if other people actually pitched in and collaborated! To be successful, you have to meet people where they are and bring them along.

Paul brought good ideas and solutions to the table, but he lacked Social Awareness. He didn't read social clues. He didn't take the time to understand where other people were coming from. He believed that good ideas would sell themselves – so he didn't develop persuasion and influencing skills. And anytime there was pushback, Paul didn't listen, he belittled. Okay, maybe Paul didn't belittle people out loud, but he definitely did....in his mind.

You see, Paul was convinced that HIS ideas and HIS perspectives were superior to others. And most of the people that Paul worked with knew that he felt this way. So, practical improvement opportunities were rejected. Potential cost-saving processes were not sustained. And worst of all, Paul was completely unaware that he was viewed as a bully.

People believed that Paul forced HIS opinions, HIS methodologies, and HIS answers on the organization – with little to no regard of the consequences or how others felt.

The cost to Paul is obvious. The real offense, however, is the negative impact that Paul's lack of awareness had on the organization, the people who worked there, and the missed opportunities. Paul made organizational improvements. Paul has the data to back up his claims, BUT... he doesn't have the Self-Awareness, Self-Management, and Social Awareness skills to truly succeed in a COptO role. In fact, Paul hasn't even begun to scratch the surface of the emotional intelligence skill sets that he would need.

Stakeholder Awareness

Stakeholders Awareness has a huge impact on a COptO role. The Stanford Research Institute defines stakeholders as "those groups without whose support the organization would cease to exist."[10] When you put that in context with a COptO, it becomes clear that stakeholders have the power to kill an idea, initiative and/or a project. That's why Chief Optimization Officers need this emotional intelligence skill to succeed.

Project management research often combines the word "management" with stakeholders. That school of thought believes that stakeholders need to be managed to mitigate risk, and they have all sorts of tools and methodologies to keep stakeholders under control.

Stakeholders don't need to be managed. They need to be heard, understood, and brought into the equation. Yes, stakeholders have the power to kill a project. However, most of them don't kill projects without good reason.

Sure, we've all known some ornery cusses that take real joy in sinking other people's initiatives. Those killjoys are not the norm, however. Most of the people we work with are reasonable human beings who are simply trying to do the right thing. But your idea and my idea of the right thing, may be very different. So, it's the COptO's job to uncover stakeholder perspectives, concerns, and ideas while being aware of and taking into consideration each stakeholder's "right thing."

Mahan Khalsa and Randy Illig have written one of our favorite books of all time; "Let's Get Real or Let's Not Play."[11] They see the world in terms of problems to be solved. And they believe that it is the consultant's responsibility to explore the space between the client's problems and the consultant's ability to identify and provide a solution.

That's exactly what a COptO must do. Chief Optimization Officers with stakeholder awareness don't come to the table armed with pre-determined solutions. They enter conversations with curiosity and a boat load of questions. They are firmly entrenched in Stephen Covey's maxim of "seek first to understand."[12] They are gathering data. They are specifically looking for what's right. And they are co-creating.

You see, stakeholder awareness is rooted in the idea that other people are brilliant. And it's the COptO's responsibility to tap into that brilliance. To build upon stakeholder experiences. To tease out stakeholder concerns. And to use the expanded perspectives of ALL stakeholders to co-create BETTER solutions, collaborating together to improve ideas.

So, if you believe you are the brightest bulb in the box... If you think the idea you developed on your own is the right answer... If you can't see merit in different perspectives... And if you don't like it when people disagree with you... You are not stakeholder aware.

Organizational Impact Awareness

The final awareness skill that Chief Optimization Officers require is Organizational Impact Awareness. Daniel Goleman, in his book Leadership that Gets Results, described Organizational Awareness as the "ability to read the currents of organizational life, build decision networks and navigate politics."[13]

Bottomline – what he is saying is that individuals who have organizational awareness have the ability to both SEE and NAVIGATE the organization's operating system.

Every organization has its own operating system. An organization's operating system is undocumented. It doesn't follow the organizational chart. It is not based upon recorded standards or mission, vision, and value statements. It IS, however, how things get done. And it consists of the complex and inter-connected relationships of:

1. Organizational structures, policies, procedures, and processes, as well as
2. Organizational relationships that are made up of human networks, patterns of power and influence, emotions, and behaviors.

An individual with organizational awareness is able to intuitively understand how the organization – as a whole – thinks, feels, and will respond to specific situations.

- They understand the organization's appetite.
- They feel the heartbeat of the organization.
- They recognize the "real" organizational landscape, not the "hoped-for" landscape.
- They get that the "right" people might not be the people with titles.
- They tap into informal networks.[14]
- And they know how to pull levers to get things done.

Meet Walter "Radar" O'Reilly.

If you don't know Radar – you are probably not a child of the 70's. Radar is a fictional character from the TV show M*A*S*H. He's always been one of our favorites – especially since his character is from Ottumwa, Iowa. Radar was the company clerk for a field hospital set against the backdrop of the Korean War. He was always surrounded by people with bigger titles and a lot more education. And he had organizational awareness.

He was called Radar because he knew things long before other people did. He had the pulse of the entire camp. He knew the people. He understood the work. And he recognized how seemingly separate roles, functions, and components – touched and impacted one another. He saw the "whole." He made decisions and took action on the "whole."

And even though he didn't have traditional military power, the entire camp aligned with his decisions. Why? Because he EARNED the privilege. He secured the camp's trust. How? His perspective, his priorities and his decisions always aligned with the "whole."

That's organizational impact awareness.

AWARENESS: Reinforcement Resources

"Experience in not what happens to you – it's how you interpret what happens to you."
– Aldous Huxley

1. If you want to learn more about YOUR Awareness Quotient, we recommend taking the Predictive Index assessment. Feel free to take this assessment and get a read back on us!

   https://assessment.predictiveindex.com/bo/E0N/COptO

2. Over the course of a week, intentionally keep track of the number of times a stakeholder tells you that something is "fine". Oh, and if you don't know what "fine" means it stands for: F&%@#! It's Not Excellent.

3. If you'd like to get some feedback, we have a great 360° feedback template at: chiefoptimizationofficer.com/tools

2

Truth Telling

"The truth is like surgery. It hurts AND it cures. A lie is like a pain killer. It gives instant relief AND it has side effects that often last forever."

— unknown

We live in a world where "truth" is elusive. On one hand we have spinners who mix facts and data with personal opinions and self-serving outcomes. On the other end of the spectrum, we have Midwest Nice where we keep opinions to ourselves to not offend.

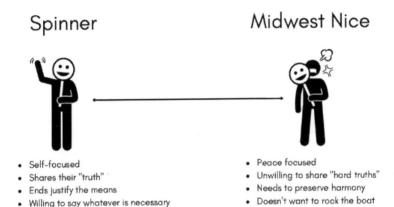

Spinner	Midwest Nice

- Self-focused
- Shares their "truth"
- Ends justify the means
- Willing to say whatever is necessary

- Peace focused
- Unwilling to share "hard truths"
- Needs to preserve harmony
- Doesn't want to rock the boat

Both ends of this spectrum suck. Both extremes erode trust. Neither one is truth telling.

Truth Telling falls somewhere in the middle. And here's the catch. You can't be an effective Truth Teller until you are trusted.

"You can't be an effective Truth Teller until you are trusted."

You see, we often kill the messenger. In fact, a Harvard study found that not only do we <u>blame</u> the messenger, we also <u>believe</u> the messenger has malicious motives. Ouch! The study also goes on to say that "would-be" messengers might want to consider "delegating the task of breaking bad news to someone else. Indeed, this may be part of the logic for hiring an HR consultancy to do firing." Wow!

Certainly, that is one alternative. May we suggest another? Instead of passing the buck when there is trouble, why not build a foundation of trustworthiness before it's needed?

Individuals who have earned the privilege of being Truth Tellers don't worry about being shot at first sight because they have laid a foundation of trust that has survived over time.

The trust equation looks like this:

$$S2D + C2 + R + F = Trustworthiness$$

Let's look at each component of the Trustworthiness Equation, one at a time.

S2D = Say-to-Do Ratio

More than 20 years ago, Tammy went to one of those weekend seminars where they basically lock you in a room and control every second of every day. Tammy hated that experience – AND she learned an extremely valuable lesson.

The trainer opened the seminar by outlining a long list of rules. One of the rules the trainer emphasized was being on time. In fact, the students were going to be punished if they broke this rule. Anyone who arrived late to the sessions or came back late from breaks had to immediately write a $100 check to their favorite charity. Then the trainer had each of the students declare their charity of choice before they moved on to the next rule.

Later in the evening when the class took their first break, lo and behold, a young man entered the room about 20 seconds after the stated deadline. True to her word, the trainer held the man accountable. She asked him why he was late. He mumbled some excuse. And after he wrote out the first punishment check of the weekend; trainer went on to provide some context.

We all make promises. We say 'yes' when our spouse asks us to pick up the dry cleaning or our boss asks if we can have that report done on Thursday. We tell our friends that we will meet them for dinner at 6pm or tell our kids that we'll pick them up from practice at 7pm. We tell ourselves we're going to start working out and lose that extra ten pounds. And we have a to-do list that we intend to get done this weekend.

Every single one of those things are promises. They are promises that we've made to others. Or they are promises that we have made to ourselves. Regardless:

When we break small promises – the ones that are easy to keep – we are more likely to break our big promises.

This statement hit Tammy like a ton of bricks. How many times had she said 'yes' to small things, without thought or intention, and didn't follow through?"

When we break promises – no matter the size – we lose credibility. We are seen as unreliable. And that's true whether we're breaking promises to others or to ourselves. In fact, the damage may be worse when we are breaking promises to ourselves.

Meet Valerie.

Valerie had a phrase that she repeated over and over for years. She would say, "I'm going to lose some weight." That mantra was a self-promise. And it was a promise she continued to break day after day, year after year.

We could debate if Valerie even NEEDED to lose weight. We could examine where her negative self-image came from. We could even give Valerie a break; after all, we do live in a very body-conscious world. Just look at how pop culture defines beauty.

For a moment, however, let's just concentrate on Valerie's self-talk. We know that when we break promises, we stand in the way of progress, we are seen as unreliable, and we lose credibility. So, what happens when we break promises to ourselves?

It turns out that the promises we make to ourselves are the most important promises we can make.

When we break promises to ourselves, we TELL ourselves that WE are UNRELIABLE. That we can't be trusted. And over time, as we continue to break our own promises, we collect evidence that PROVES we can't trust OURSELVES.

> "When we break promises to ourselves, we TELL ourselves that WE are unreliable."

Imagine for a moment the labels we may put on ourselves enable our belief that we can't trust ourselves. Labels like weak, stupid, lazy, and undisciplined. Peg O'Connor, a professor at Gustavus Adolphus College, wrote in a Psychology Today article that second-guessing, waffling, changing course, deferring to others, and self-sabotage are all behaviors that can be traced back to a lack of self-trust.[15]

To be in relationship, with ourselves and with others...
To trust ourselves and others...

We need to have a long history of keeping our promises. In other words, we need a high Say-to-Do Ratio (S2D).

Our S2D Ratio is calculated by dividing the promises we keep by the promises we make.

No one has a 100% S2D Ratio. Having that kind of expectation or setting the bar that high is unreasonable. Our S2D Ratio, however, is the foundation of trustworthiness. It determines whether we have earned the right to be a truth teller. Without a high score – our words won't carry any weight.

Ralph Waldo Emerson once said: "*Your actions speak so loudly, I cannot hear what you are saying.*" Actions speak louder than words. So, if you want to be a Truth Teller... If you don't want to be killed when you deliver hard truths to power.

If you want to truly serve the organization and the people that work there, and not be seen as self-serving. You need a S2D Ratio that is greater than 90%.

C2 = Competence & Contribution

Competence and contribution are the next components of Trustworthiness. Without both, people won't trust you. They may like you. They may enjoy your company. They may even think you're funny. They won't, however, trust you.

Tammy is a volleyball player. Her job as the setter is to take the second touch and deliver it to a hitter so that they can get a kill. She loves watching the moment the ball and the hitter align perfectly. And she feels a huge sense of accomplishment and camaraderie when the ball blasts off the floor on the OTHER side of the net.

People that Tammy played with would tell you that she knew the game, was willing to outwork the competition, and that she pulled her weight...until she turned 55. That's when this Competence & Contribution lesson came to life.

As Tammy's knees eroded, she found that her teammates still enjoyed her company and cared for her. However, they no longer trusted that she could deliver the ball to the hitter on a consistent basis. Tammy hated that. And they were right.

Of course, no one SAID anything. They just kept compensating for her lack of skill... until they started losing on a consistent basis. And then, Tammy could see it – the lack of trust and respect in their eyes. And she experienced it – they no longer wanted to hear what she had to say – at least on the court. Tammy knew they loved her – as a person. As a teammate, well that was another story.

Tammy was not pulling her weight. Tammy was no longer competent. Tammy was no longer contributing at the same level as the rest of the team. And Tammy was keeping THE TEAM from reaching their goals and their potential. Therefore, her perspectives, her point of view, and even her understanding of the game didn't have the same value as it had before.

Without competence and contribution, an individual's "truth" is not welcomed.

> "Without competency and contribution, an individual's "truth" is not welcomed."

R = Relationship

Do you remember what it was like when you were about eight years old? Scott remembers hanging out with the entire neighborhood playing kickball and freeze tag. It didn't matter who you were. If you showed up you were included. Scott loved that time in his life. All he had to do was be there and smile – and he was in relationship.

Adult relationships are different. People would look at us cock-eyed if we asked someone if they wanted to be our friend. And because cynicism comes with age – many people might automatically assume you "want" something. Yet, to be a Truth Teller you must be in relationship. And good relationships are two-way streets.

To "earn a relationship, you must go first." And you must be "willing to first make an investment in relationship in order to earn and deserve the relationship."[16]

We received a call the other day from a peer association group. They had held their first post-COVID networking meeting and unfortunately, it bombed. They thought people would be excited about seeing one another after months of virtual meetings. And they were.

But maybe a few of the attendees were a tad bit too excited. The meeting organizers actually described the experience as a "feeding frenzy."

You see, there are people who joined the association because they wanted to connect with their peers and grow their professional skills. And there are consultants who joined the association to build relationships and sell their services to the first group. We are sure by now you can imagine what happened.

After 15 months of isolation, the consultants were overly eager. And to give them a bit of a break, they were completely willing to go first! They initiated conversations. And they made sure no one was left alone. Their actions aligned with The Trusted Advisor's concept of to "earn a relationship, you must go first." The problem was that they either ignored or misinterpreted the second point, that you need to invest in a relationship to earn it.

Bob Burg and John David Mann, the authors of *The Go-Giver: A Little Story About a Powerful Business Idea*,[17] described investing in and earning a relationship this way. They said you need to:
1. Give more value than you receive
2. Serve others – really well
3. Place other people's interests first
4. Offer the most valuable gift you have – your true self

The consultants at this networking meeting made the cardinal mistake of putting their personal and professional needs ahead of the individuals they wanted to be in relationship with. They were SELLING and selling hard when the most important thing they could have done was GIVE and give well and freely.

One of the workshops we facilitate (which is why the association phoned us) is called "Optimizing Your Networking." Too often, individuals are sent to networking events and told to collect business cards. Honestly – we can't think of a better example of "wasted excellence." We believe that networking is an opportunity to GIVE first. And during our workshop, we show people how to initiate conversations by asking questions to discover who the other individual is and how they might best serve them.

When you serve others first:
- Your actions demonstrate that you want to be in relationship.
- Your investment in them establishes that you have positive intentions.
- Your good work and work ethic proves that you have integrity.

Adult working relationships don't just happen because you show up and smile. You have to earn the relationship. And you MUST invest in and earn the relationship before you tap that relationship and ask for something in return.

Oh, and one last thing. If you are in relationship, you don't keep score. You just keep following Burg and Mann's four steps – and then accept their fifth step: Be open to receiving!

F = Forgiveness

We've all been in relationships where trust has been broken. In some cases, the relationship is destroyed forever. In others, people are able to work through it and the relationship gets stronger.

What made the difference? Time and forgiveness.

Time is not necessarily our friend. Yes, some people need a bit of time to think things through before they address a difficult issue. A "bit of time" however is very different from a few weeks, a couple of months or a bunch of years. When there is a problem – we need to address it sooner rather than later. Why? Because of this ugly thing called resentment. The longer we wait, the more resentment we may feel.

We worked with a state agency a few years ago and remember when one of the participants talked very animatedly about his experience with a superior. As he was sharing, all of his peers were nodding their heads in agreement – which we interpreted as "yes, this is the way it is at this organization."

Naively, we asked a question: "When did this happen?". His answer: "10 years ago."

WHAT?

Betrayals, disagreements, pain, and even perceived slights are not like wine. They do not get better with time. Just ask the Hatfields and the McCoys.

Time often magnifies the problem. And the longer we delay working through it, the bigger the gap. To make things worse, the next time something happens, we tend to look at it through the lens of the previous unresolved issue. That means we will have a negative bias. And we will struggle giving the other person the benefit of the doubt because we are holding on to "what's wrong."

When you play this out for a few weeks (let alone a couple of months or many years) you'll find that these unresolved issues will result in building a wall between you and the other person. Not only will you end up not trusting them, worse than that, you may no longer want them to succeed. In fact, you may be so resentful that you might privately wish they would get what (you think) they deserve.

When that happened to us, we finally understood. TIME was the real enemy. When we let too much time pass, we became ill-intentioned. That's ugly. AND, so easy to avoid. All it takes is the courage to step up to the plate and have the conversation. Forgiveness IS possible if you don't wait too long.

It's also important to remember that everyone will make a mistake. Everyone will screw up. Everyone. That includes you!

If you're alive, you're a screw-up. That is just the way it is. So, if you hold grudges, have a memory like an elephant, or for some reason or another think that people aren't allowed to make mistakes – YOU will be the one that suffers.

Why? Because if you hold others to impossible standards – others will hold you to the same standards. And you'll never measure up.

So, what do we really mean when we're talking about forgiveness? Think about it this way. We're not talking about forgiving:

- The individual who refuses to align with the organization.
- The person who continually lies, steals and cheats.
- The team member who hasn't learned to take responsibility, points fingers and blames

everyone but themselves.

- The leader who repeatedly puts their own needs above the organization and/or the people he or she serves.

These are not situations where we need to worry about forgiveness. These individuals have demonstrated a pattern of behavior – over time – and they need to be shown the door. They don't belong in your organization. And if they stay – they will bring the entire company down to their level.

What we are talking about is forgiving one another when we are simply being human. Let's face it. Human beings make mistakes.

According to Leadership and Self-Deception by the Arbinger Group, we're all a little blind and we've all made mistakes.[18] Think about a recent time when you screwed up.

Maybe you were:
- Angry and said the wrong thing.
- Self-centered and pushed your own agenda.
- Stubborn and didn't want to listen.
- Forceful and rammed your solutions down everyone else's throats.
- Arrogant and unwilling to consider different perspectives.
- Scared and didn't speak up.

- Blind and was unwilling to see.
- Busy and overlooked all the signs.
- Too focused on one thing and ignored something important.
- Ignorant and made the wrong call.
- Being stupid and in that moment made a bad decision.

We've all been there. We've all done that. The questions we must ask ourselves are:

1. Is this behavior typical?
2. Does this individual demonstrate this behavior repeatedly?
3. Can we see a pattern?
4. Or is this a one-off?

We all have areas of growth that we need to pay attention to. We all will screw up once in a while. And we need to recognize the difference between a once-in-a-blue-moon blow-up and a repeat offender.

Occasional mistakes need to be forgiven and forgotten. We need to let go of the small stuff. We need to extend grace. And we need to practice memory loss.

We don't want to be remembered for our worst day. We want to be remembered for our <u>FULL body of work</u>. We are willing to take the good with the bad – because we believe our good outweighs our bad. Ultimately, we believe that if we are judged by the contributions we have made, the way we typically behave and treat others, and the energy and innovation we have brought to the table – we will receive a passing mark. If, however, our worst day erases the rest of our days – we wouldn't stand a chance. And neither would you. ☹

We all deserve to be judged on our full body of work. And if you want to be a Truth Teller you will have to earn that privilege by letting go of the small stuff, addressing the big stuff in a timely manner, extending grace, and practicing memory loss.

Being a Truth Teller is a tall order. And it's a baseline requirement. If you hope to be a successful COptO you must master this equation:

$$\frac{\textbf{S2D} \text{ (Say-to-Do Ratio)}}{} $$

S2D (Say-to-Do Ratio)

C^2 (Competence and Contribution)

R (Relationship)

+ **F** (Forgiveness)
_____

Trustworthiness

Trustworthiness EARNS you the PRIVILEDGE to be a Truth Teller.

TRUTH TELLING
Reinforcement Resources
"Telling someone the truth is a loving act."
– Mal Pancoast

1. Over the course of two weeks, track your S2D Ratio.

   o What promises did you make to others?
   o What promises did you make to yourself?
   o How many promises did you break?
   o How many promises did you keep?
   o Calculate your S2D Ratio
   o What did you learn?

2. Are you a Truth Teller? Or do you avoid the truth? Pay attention over the course of 30 days. How many times did you tell your truth – kindly? How many times did you wait to tell your truth until you were angry? And how many times did you simply not speak up?

3

Curiousness

"The mind that opens to a new idea, never returns to its original size."

— Albert Einstein

We recently used a well-known tool called a nine box with one of our clients. They had spent the last 18 months developing their middle managers and wanted to have a frank discussion about each manager's current performance and their perceived potential.

Typical 9-Box

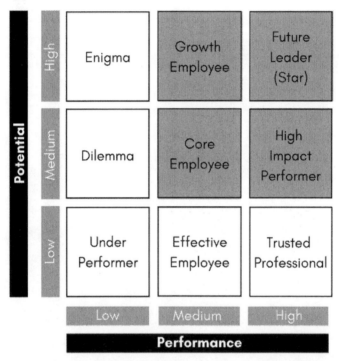

As we worked together to place each manager on this grid, the team kept going back and wrestling with the concept of potential.

They had already "agreed" on the criteria they would use to evaluate potential, but it wasn't working. At least, not until we suggested replacing the word "potential" with "curiousness".

9-Box with Curiousness

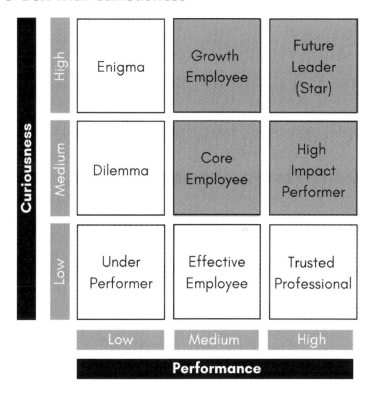

Egon Zehnder, a consulting and executive search firm, suggests that you cannot have potential without curiosity.[19]

Why?

"You cannot have potential
without curiosity."

Tammy's first consulting client was an insurance company in Des Moines, Iowa. They were growing by leaps and bounds and needed to level up their frontline and middle managers. So, they asked her to design and facilitate a leadership academy. It was a great first gig! Designing the curriculum was interesting. Working with and developing the organization's leaders over the course of seven years was awesome. AND, learning from the person who hired Tammy was priceless. Her name was Betty.

Betty attended every minute of every session for seven years.

Tammy remembers her telling an old Chinese proverb that went something like this.

A Chinese master was having tea with his students. When he went to refill a guest's teacup he did not stop when the cup was full, and the tea spilled out onto the table and then ran onto the floor.

Many of the students raised their voices to tell their master to stop. "The cup is full."

The old master calmly put down the tea pot and said, "exactly." "Many of you are just like this cup – full of ideas. You come and ask for teaching and wisdom, but your cup is full. I cannot teach you until you make room in your cup."

Making room in our cups is harder than it sounds. Most of us have been taught that we need to be the person with answers. And as we progress in our careers, this urge to be knowledgeable – competent – only becomes more prevalent. Unfortunately, increased competence often goes along with reduced curiosity. In fact, the research indicates that curiosity declines the longer we are in a job.[20]

Meet Professor Robert S. Langer

Bob is a very unique human being. We have actually never met Bob, AND we have always wanted to.

- Google Scholar lists Bob as the most cited engineer of all time – with more than 346,000 citations.
- Bob has more than 1,400 patents (issued and pending). Four hundred of those patents have been licensed or sublicensed.
- Bob is one of only twelve Institute Professors at MIT.

What is an Institute Professor? It's an honor bestowed by MIT Faculty and Administration to colleagues who have "demonstrated exceptional distinction by a combination of leadership, accomplishment, and service in the scholarly, educational, and general intellectual life of the Institute or wider academic community." [21]

And, in his spare time, Bob is an author with more than 1,500 published articles.

With all those accomplishments, however, our favorite thing about Bob is that what he really wants to do is "help people make the transition from GIVING good answers to ASKING good questions."[22] And, while, Bob is MUCH smarter than we are and WAY more accomplished, Bob and Tammy have something in common.

For more than 27 years Tammy has led a workshop called "Extreme Facilitation." Tammy landed on the word "extreme" very purposely and LONG before it was a buzz word. This five-day, all-day (yes, you read that correctly) course enables participants to transition from being a trainer to being a facilitator.

What's the difference between training and facilitating?

It's the shift from GIVING good answers to ASKING powerful questions! It's the modification from being the expert to enabling others to become experts. It's the adjustment in one's thinking from believing YOU have the answers to empowering OTHERS to discover answers.

You see, the myth is that we need to have answers if we want to be trusted and respected. The truth, however, is that individuals who are curious are MORE respected.[23] And individuals who make room for others have the opportunity to make curiousness go viral.

Imagine for a minute a team where people:

- Believe that their colleagues' perspectives have merit.
- Bring half-baked ideas and work product to the table.
- Go out of their way to ask one another for input.
- Purposefully pull together brain trusts to evaluate ideas.
- Debate with passion while at the same time listening intently.
- Ensure that all of the thinking behind a suggestion is understood.
- Consider what's right about ideas and advice.
- Mull over and play around with input for a while.
- And then, take action.

That's the Pixar process. And they have institutionalized curiousness.[24]

It starts with leaders who model the way. Ed Catmull, Pixar's co-founder, has found that the fundamental skill of curiousness is the ability to have "very intense and heated discussions." These passionate conversations are about making the movie (you could insert product, system, process here) better while there is still time to shift gears. And it doesn't matter who provides the feedback. Great directors (you could insert leaders here) "appreciate all contributions, regardless of where or from whom they originate, and use the best ones."

These "heated" discussions can work – but only if we turn off our "I'm right" bias and consider other perspectives and data. And that is way actually more difficult than you might realize.

By the time we reach adulthood, we are so full of information and opinions that we don't even notice they are there. We might consider ourselves to be open-minded, but in fact, everything we learn is filtered through multiple assumptions and then classified to fit into the knowledge we already possess. That's why we need what Julia Galef calls the Scout Mindset.

In her book of that title, Galef argues that most of us have a "Soldier's Mindset."[25] We defend our positions. A scout, on the other hand, is out front "mapping the terrain, identifying potential obstacles," and above all, discovering what is "really out there as accurately as possible."

Scouts are curious. When they encounter something that contradicts their thinking, they are intrigued. And they are flexible and adaptable. Their self-worth is not dependent on being right. So, as more information and data become available, Scouts update their perspective. They have no need to hold on to outdated thinking.[26]

Curious individuals:

1. Embrace Bob Langer's perspective about asking great questions.
2. Recognize it is not about what THEY know, it's about what OTHERS discover.
3. Institutionalize collective curiousness.
4. Choose to have a Scout Mindset.

AND, they have a much better chance of growing into the C-Suite.[27]

CURIOUSNESS
Reinforcement Resources

"Curiosity is the fuel for discovery, inquiry, and learning."

— Anonymous

1. How do the words potential and curiousness apply to you?

2. How full is YOUR cup?

3. Over the course of the next few weeks, track how many times you ask a question versus provide someone with an answer. What did you notice?

4. How did you feel about heated, passionate discussions? What could you do to become more comfortable when people disagree?

4
GATHERER

"Nothing is more important than being a gatherer of good ideas and information. That's called doing your homework."

— Jim Rohn

Hunter-Gatherer

Many of us may not relate to the concept of hunter gatherer. Let's face it, most of us stopped hunting and gathering 12,000 years ago. And the hunter-gatherer societies that are left, well, they are barely surviving.[28]

So, what could we possibly learn from their example?

We would suggest that hunter-gatherer societies employed a necessary skill set that is very applicable to organizations today. They foraged. The research indicates that most hunter-gatherer adults spent two hours a day collecting the wild plants and animals they needed to sustain themselves and the other members of their tribe.[29]

Most of us would say that we're happy to live in a world where we don't have to scavenge for raspberries or shoot bunnies to feed our families. However, we still need to forage. We simply need to hunt for and gather different things.

What do we need to gather? Well, Scott would say "that depends". And of course, he is right. It DOES depend – on your role in the organization. For instance – salespeople need to gather relationships, leads, and deals. Frontline customer service representatives need to gather technical knowledge and EQ skills. And we would suggest that COptOs need to gather ideas, information, and data, as well as people, perspectives, and input. Think of it this way. The opposite of gathering is scattering.

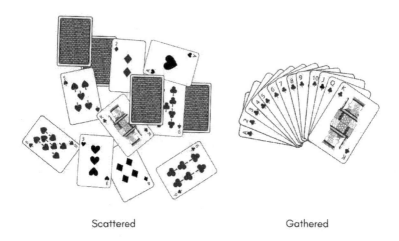

Scattered   Gathered

Ideas, people, and connections are scattered across the organization. A COptO needs to first see that the ideas and people are OUT there (remember Julia Galef's Scout Mindset in Chapter 3), and then gather and connect them to benefit the organization.

A successful Chief Optimization Officer needs to gather THREE types of things:

- *Ideas*, information, and data.
- *People*, perspectives, and input.
- *Connections*, How the two above fit together

"Ideas, people, and connections are scattered across the organization."

Human Business Model

This dual perspective fits perfectly into something we call the Human Business Model. And most of us prefer one perspective over the other.

Case in point.

In our relationship, Scott excels at the business side of the equation. He is an electromagnet –, attracting ideas, information, data, and technical methodologies like they are going out of style. He sees and thinks things through at the speed of light and typically from a technical, process-oriented and results-oriented outlook.

That foundation attracts MORE ideas, information and data, and Scott is then able to take all of that and reorient it so that it makes sense – making something simple that is bigger and even better than the sum of its parts.

Tammy, on the other hand, relates more to the human side of the equation. So, if Scott is an electromagnet, Tammy is a people-magnet. She meets people wherever she goes. And they often have surprisingly interesting conversations.

Tammy learned about politics from a White House intern when they were stuck together on an airplane on the tarmac at Washington National Airport for six hours. While Tammy was grocery shopping, she found out that if you have any chances of winning, you need to blow dry a sow's hair before you show her at the fair. And of course, who hasn't had the experience of meeting someone on the golf course who could teach you all about crab fishing in the Bering Sea?

So, while most of us have a preference, human-over-business or business-over-human, a COptO needs to consciously and purposefully attract and pay attention to both sides of the equation. If not, what they gather will be out of balance. And the result will be solutions that satisfy one side over the other.

Let's play that idea out for a moment. What would happen if all our solutions were geared towards taking care of people? What could possibly be wrong with that?

Hey - don't get us wrong. We're all in for taking care of the people who do the work and get results. AND, sometimes an organization will HAVE TO ask their people to give MORE to get the results they need. Think about meeting client deadlines, saying yes to an opportunity that will REALLY stretch the organization, or pivoting to respond to something completely unforeseen — like COVID-19. Sometimes an organization needs to put BUSINESS first to ensure the sustainability of the organization.

Now, for the other side of the coin. What happens when our solutions are always geared towards results — taking care of the bottom line? What's wrong with that?

Again, we're all in for building lucrative businesses. If, however, an organization is willing to consistently sacrifice its employees at the altar of profitability, they will more than likely have a workforce issue!

We've been around long enough to remember the 2010 employment predictions. Back then, the employment research was looking at Baby Boomer retirements, and the best minds of the day predicted that there would be deficit of more than 10 million employees. Then 2008 and the mortgage crisis happened. The stock market took a nosedive, baby boomers didn't retire, and we ended up with an abundance of talent in the marketplace. When talent is readily available, some organizations may be able to afford a revolving employee door – until they can't.

Let's look at an organization we'll call Bottom Line Always (BLA). BLA is a tech company. They have smart, talented, and visionary leaders. Early in the organization's history, they saw an opportunity and immediately developed a great business-to-business (B2B) solution. It didn't take long for the marketplace to respond. Almost immediately BLA was realizing a 20-30 percent growth rate year over year. Awesome. Who wouldn't want that? But there was a downside. BLA was also experiencing a turnover rate that was significant. In fact, at the time it was almost three times higher than their tech cohorts. Ouch!

BLA's leadership was not worried about their turnover. They saw the world from the results side of the Human Business Model. And talent, at the time, was plentiful.

By BLA's tenth year in business they were hiring hundreds of new employees annually and had opened offices in multiple states. That sounds good. And the story the BLA executives were telling themselves was that they needed to expand into other states to find good talent. The word on the street, however, was "don't work for BLA, they are a burn and churn company."

The talent was readily available locally. It's just that the local talent didn't want to work for BLA. It is too early to tell you how BLA is faring in 2021 as the country is experiencing #TheBIGShift and #TheGreatResignation. But we think you can guess!

Successful COptOs need to gather both people, perspectives, and input – the human side of the equation AND ideas, information, and data – the business side of the equation. Think about it like a healthy diet – COptOs need a healthy balance of both.

Life Long Learners

Hunter-gatherers spent two hours a day – consistently – foraging for what they needed. COptO's need to do the same. They don't wait for a crisis. They don't wait until they are REALLY hungry.

To be successful, gathering needs to become part of a COptO's daily routine.

Gathering is a discovery process and you never really know what you're going to find or where you are going to find it.

It could be that:
- Someone stopped you with a question which made you curious enough to look into it.
- You read about a time-saving hack on LinkedIn.
- You found a tasty tidbit as you were wandering through a trade magazine.
- A colleague brought an idea to you.
- You showed up for a regularly scheduled Zoom meeting with a long-term professional colleague.
- A person in a class you were taking or facilitating said something profound.
- You were talking with a person you just met, and they asked a great question that sparked a lightbulb moment.
- A Netflix movie sparked an idea.
- You took the time to tour another organization's facility.

"Gathering needs to become part of a COptO's daily routine."

Consistent discovering leads to life-long-learning. And life-long-learning has some amazing personal benefits including increased self-confidence, fatter paychecks, and improved interpersonal relationships. On the business side, life-long-learning actually improves resiliency and enables organizations to more readily adapt to change – including technical changes.[30]

Proactively gathering ensures you are prepared when an opportunity or crisis hits.

GATHERER

Reinforcement Resources

"Ideas, people, and connections are scattered across the organization. It is our responsibility to gather and connect them to benefit the organization"

– Chief Optimization Officer

1. How do you go about gathering? Are you effective? Do you gather all the time or only when you need something?

2. What side of the equation do you prefer? Human or Business?

3. What habits do you have that prove that you are a life-long learner? What else could you do? Choose one additional life-long learning habit. What is it? And how are you going to practice it – consistently?

5
RUTHLESS DISCERNMENT

"The difference between successful people and really successful people is that really successful people say no to almost everything."

— Warren Buffett

Not everything is created equal.

Yes, we've read the Declaration of Independence – and we don't think Thomas Jefferson took the words "All men are created equal" literally. He knew, and we know, that people do not have the "same" physical characteristics, emotional make-up, and intellectual capabilities.

The same holds true for ideas and opportunities. 99.9% of the time, ideas and opportunities are not equal to one another.

"99.9% of the time, ideas and opportunities are not equal to one another."

And here's the tricky part.

If we were to compare two people, or two ideas, or two opportunities – there may not be a CLEAR winner. Each will have its own merits. Each will have a downside. And one may not "beat" the other. Now what do we do?

We define discernment as the ability to successfully perceive, judge, distinguish, and decide. And we believe that discernment may well be the most overlooked and under-appreciated leadership competency of the 21st century.

> "Discernment may well be the most overlooked and under-appreciated leadership competency of the 21st century."

Misinformation

Think about misinformation for a minute. Regardless of your political viewpoint, we can agree that:
- Social media and even mainstream media can be misleading.
- Data can be manipulated to support a specific point of view.
- Organizations often measure what's easy instead of measuring what's meaningful.
- Many people have difficulty putting numbers in context.

Sometimes we are fed misinformation. And sometimes we are our own source of misinformation. We want to believe what we want to believe.

We see this a lot in traditional strategic planning. Many organizations start with a SWOT analysis (Strengths, Weaknesses, Opportunities and Threats). When considering strengths, the intent is to identify what the organization does BETTER than their competitors. They should be looking for their unique differentiators. But too often, they look at their performance with a set of very rosy glasses. They're not looking at the information with a discerning eye. They are looking at the data with prejudice. And they measure progress instead of differentiators. They say things like: "We're sooo much better than "last quarter" or "last year" or when "so and so led the organization."

That is not discernment. It is misinformation of our own making. We are fooling ourselves.

"Sometimes we are fed misinformation. Sometimes we are our own source of misinformation."

If we want to be ruthlessly discerning, we must set aside the "stories" that we want to tell ourselves. We must look at ourselves in the mirror and see what we truly are. The complete 360-degree view. Not what we wish we were. Not who we "used" to be. And not just all our faults and foibles.

We need to be willing to COMPLETE the picture. To listen to both our good and bad press. To look for the obvious and the not-so-obvious. And to consider what we know and what we may not know.

Individuals who are ruthlessly discerning don't take the easy road and don't settle for easy answers. They push further, dig deeper, and contemplate an even bigger and broader landscape.

> "Individuals who are ruthlessly discerning don't take the easy road and don't settle for the easy answers. They push further, dig deeper and contemplate an even bigger and broader landscape."

Polarized Thinking

For many of us, it is comfortable to see the world in black or white. Something is right or wrong, good or bad, safe or dangerous.

That's what our educational system taught and reinforced in us. There IS a right answer. 2 + 2 = 4. Period. And when we gave our teachers the correct answers we were rewarded with good grades. So, we didn't go searching for another right answer. The ONE answer was all we needed.

Unfortunately, life may not be that simple. Consider for a moment that two different – even opposite – truths can exist at the same time.

- It's a great solution AND a crappy solution.
- There is strength in our weakness.
- We are very good AND we're not good enough.

When we can hold on to two opposite ideas at the same time, things are no longer good OR bad. We are not stuck in polarization. And we won't believe there is one perfect answer. There are many answers. There are a multitude of methodologies. And we will find ourselves asking questions like: "what don't we understand?" or "what are we missing?"

This kind of thinking and questioning expands our reality. It allows us to think bigger, consider broader perspectives, and make better decisions. This is the realization that hits every successful leader at one point or another in their careers. And without it, an individual is not ready to assume the mantle of executive responsibility.

Tammy learned this powerful lesson when she was 42. Tammy was part of a five-member leadership team that was tasked with building an organization from the ground up.

They had a B2B product, an expansion plan, and fortunately for them, a decent amount of start-up capital. One of her responsibilities was hiring and training technicians.

Their plan called for opening three locations every quarter. That meant Tammy had to find and train six technicians at a time. And honestly, she loved this work. Finding the right people, giving them the foundation to succeed, and watching them go from newbies to skilled technicians was one of the joys of her professional life.

And then Tammy hired Francis.

Francis was just one of those individuals that you are drawn to. He was smart, witty, optimistic, and met all the base qualifications. Tammy just KNEW he was something special. And her gut said that HE was going to end up as a leader in the organization.

On day one, Francis pulled up in his spotless F150 pickup and was ready to go. He filled out his paperwork and headed off to the training center with a big smile on his face. By Thursday evening the organization's Master Technician was convinced Francis was going to be our next regional lead tech. Francis was miles ahead of the standard learning curve. He was a natural with the equipment. He worked his butt off. He asked all the right questions.

He made connections between specific techniques and outcomes. AND, he helped his cohorts.

Four days into a 10-day training program this start-up had found a regional leader. Yippee!

Then, on Friday morning, the HR Generalist came to Tammy with an issue. She had asked Francis for his driver's license a couple of times earlier in the week, and Francis had continued to put her off. Tammy immediately got a very sick feeling in the pit of her stomach. All the techs would be driving a company van, so a valid driver's license was a requirement of the job. And Tammy KNEW she had asked Francis about his driving record during the initial phone interview.

So, Tammy did what every respectable Vice President of Human Resources would do. She went outside and peeked in the window of his shiny F150 pickup. And there it was, an ignition breathalyzer. Francis had to blow into that contraption every time he wanted to drive somewhere. His truck wouldn't start unless he didn't have any alcohol in his system. And now Tammy knew for a fact that Francis had flat-out lied in his interview about his driving record.

We are guessing many of you would have fired Francis on the spot. Tammy didn't.

The road that Francis and Tammy traveled together that day was not easy. Over the course of about three hours, Tammy asked a lot of questions and Francis decided to come clean. She learned that Francis was an alcoholic. He had three DWI convictions. He'd spent some time in prison. And he'd lied about all of it on his resume and in our interviews.

ALL very good reasons to fire Francis.

Tammy also learned from her Master Technician that Francis had aced his first four practicum tests and based on the metrics, he was their #1 trainee of all time. In addition, his behavior scores were top-notch. He showed up, on time. He did what he was asked to do. He got along well with his co-trainees. He looked for ways to improve his technical skills. And when there was downtime, he found ways to add value, like cleaning the equipment and organizing the work site.

ALL very good reasons for keeping Francis.

Yes, Francis was a problem. AND, he was a hardworking individual who had the ability to do the work that needed to be done. Francis was not one OR the other. He was not good OR bad. He was both at the same time.

Francis was still with the organization when Tammy left two years later. He became the organization's Master Technician and Trainer. And fast forward to 2021. He's been clean and sober for more than 18 years!

Micro vs Macro Decisions

Francis' story had a happy ending, but it could have just as easily gone south. And if we concentrate on what's the worst that can happen, we tend to make MACRO decisions in situations where we could make MICRO decisions.

A micro decision is simply a small-scale or short-term decision. It's a way of saying, "let's try something simple, fast and cheap – and see what happens."

Tammy made a series of micro decisions with Francis that allowed them to move forward, one step at a time. The investment of time, money, and resources at each micro decision was relatively minor. The organization was not betting the house or putting all their eggs in one basket. They were conducting a series of small experiments. There was very little risk associated with each step. And at the conclusion of each step, the organization had the opportunity to evaluate if they wanted to continue or not.

We all know individuals who make a decision thinking it is a macro decision when actually it is a micro decision - someone who turns down an interview because they don't meet one of the qualifications listed in the job description. Or an employee that says no to a special project because it didn't come with a pay raise. When we inflate decisions and make them bigger than they need to be – we miss out on the learning and wisdom that comes from making smaller, less risky decisions.

And interestingly enough, if we're constantly making macro decisions, we'd better be right – otherwise we actually might be betting the house!

Saying No

Ruthless discernment always means saying no more often than saying yes.

We'd love to tell you that Francis was the only "questionable" hire Tammy and that start up organization made, but that wouldn't be honest. They hired almost 80 technicians. 27% of those hires were asked to leave before they finished their 10-day training program. Another 4% didn't make it through their 90-day probationary period.

Tammy was never concerned with those numbers.

She knew that the organization's success was dependent on the technician's customer service and technical skills. And if the organization didn't say no to individuals who did not meet their standards, it would lead to disaster.

"Ruthless discernment always means saying no more often than saying yes."

EVERY hire was THAT important. So, Tammy and the organization said no, frequently.

- They said no to moody individuals who had great technical skills.
- They said no to people with plenty of energy who didn't pay attention to details.
- They said no to characters who wouldn't show up on time.
- They said no to the personalities that couldn't get along with others.
- And they said no to people who needed someone to tell them what do to next.

Each one of the individuals they said no to, was a vampire. Vampires suck more resources out of the system than they add. And when you devote resources to things that don't add value – you no longer have the resources you need for the things that do add value.

"Vampires suck *more* resources out of the system than they add."

Most organizations don't have resources that they can waste. They have a limited number of hours. They have a finite amount of capital. Due dates and deadlines need to be met. And people resources like knowledge, drive, energy, and motivation can be easily squandered.

That's why you need to embrace saying no.

- When you say no to okay ideas...
- When you say no to "C" players...
- When you say no to projects that aren't in the middle of your hit zone...
- When you say no to clients and customers that are not a good fit...

You make room for and have the capacity for what IS right and what DOES fit – and then you succeed. Why? Because you made room for the best and got rid of the rest.

RUTHLESS DISCERNMENT

Reinforcement Resources

"Focus means saying no to the 100 other good ideas."

– Steve Jobs

1. For a week, track your decisions. In reflection:
   - What trends and themes do you see?
   - What is the difference between your yeses and your nos?
   - Are there things to which you could have or should have said no? Why didn't you?

2. Do you want to know if you have a vampire in your life? Take our free vampire assessment

   chiefoptimizationofficer.com/tools

3. How are your vampires impacting results? What are you going to do about it?

6

HOLISTIC PERSPECTIVE

"Improving the performance of the parts of a system taken separately will not necessarily improve the performance of the whole; in fact, it may harm the whole."

— Russell Ackoff

The Cheshire Cat in Lewis Carroll's Alice in Wonderland pointed out, "If you don't know where you are going, any road will take you there."[31] And that's okay if the place you land is not important and you have the resources to wander, discover, and explore.

We've actually gone on meandering vacations where we let daily circumstances dictate our choices. There came a time however, when our destination became critically important. We wanted and needed to make it back home.

Organizationally there is a time to wander, discover, and explore. That's what Gathering (Chapter 4) is all about. Then there's a time to decide. That's Ruthless Discernment (Chapter 5). And when that decision needs to be put in context, that's when a holistic perspective is necessary and needed.

Start with the End in Mind

Holistic perspectives start with the end in mind, and the game of golf provides the perfect illustration.

Many amateur golfers' number one concern is distance. So, as they play each hole, they choose a club that will allow them to hit the ball as far as they can – without going over the green. They believe distance equals fewer swings. Pro golfers approach the game very differently.

Distance is not the goal. Maximizing the potential of every shot is the goal. So, they don't play a hole from tee to green. They play "backwards" from green to tee.[32]

Let us explain.

An amateur would typically begin by choosing a club for distance. They want to hit the ball as far down the right-hand side of the fairway as possible, hoping to get a clear shot at the green so they don't have to shoot over the sand bunkers on their second shot. If they hit the ball far enough, they can safely two putt for a total of four on this hole.

In contrast, the pro starts by considering where the hole is on the green. They determine where the ball needs to land on the green so that it will set them up for a one putt. Once that decision is made, they identify where the ball needs to land in the fairway so that they can place their second shot exactly where they want it on the green. Once these two decisions are made, the pro pulls out the club they need to position their fairway shot in the perfect place. An average pro will take a three on this hole. If good fortune is with them – they could end up with a two. Oh, and just in case you didn't know, the lower your score in golf, the better!

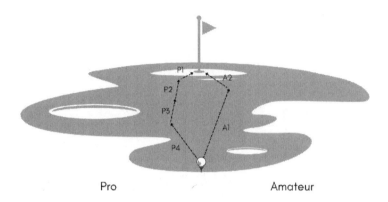

Pro   Amateur

This process of starting with the end in mind applies in all sorts of situations.

Consider the benefits of starting with the end in mind:

- Before you choose your mate or spend your paycheck.
- Before you have a difficult conversation.
- When you know what you want to achieve.
- When you can name the goal.
- When you can define success.

Then you can put things in context and begin to see how things are interrelated. And that allows you to maximize the potential of each decision along the way.

Let's look at an example.

The state had subsidized a local attraction for many years. But when the state needed to tighten its belt, the organization could see the writing on the wall. Historically the organization had focused on service, believing that if they provided superior service to their daily visitors, people would continue to come. That had always been enough; however, the problem was that without subsidies, customer revenues were not enough to keep the organization's head above water.

When the state gave the organization a two-year heads-up that their subsidies were going to be eliminated, the CEO and board agreed on a strategy of innovation. The issue? Innovation was not in the organization's DNA. So, leadership immediately mobilized and started with the end in mind by defining what innovative success looked like.

They determined that "Innovative Success" would:
- Secure grants.
- Attract additional visitors.
- Introduce new revenue streams.
- Reduce costs.

Preference would be given to ideas that tapped into two or more of these success factors. Now all they had to do was prepare the organization for a very different journey.

Building the Bridge

Any time an organization shifts, it's important to remember that what got you here is not what is going to get you there. Something must fundamentally change if an organization is going to end up at a different destination. So, what needs to be different?

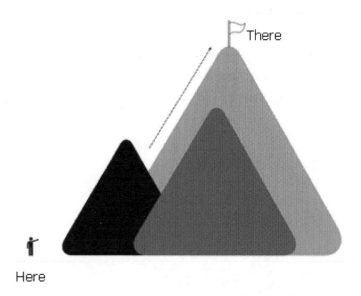

Here are some of the questions this organization asked that enabled them to build the bridge:

- What resources do we have today? How could we deploy those resources differently?
- How much revenue do we need to raise, by when?

- What capabilities/skill sets will we need to reach our goals? What behaviors will we need to reach our goals? What policies will we need to put in place to reward the right behaviors?
- How do our hiring practices need to be modified? What compensation system needs to be put in place to attract the needed skills sets?
- What leadership systems do we need to put in place to support staff?
- What organizational structure will enable the organization to achieve success? How will our current departments be impacted? Where will resources need to be deployed differently?
- How will we measure success? How will we reward success?
- What training will be needed?
- What should our internal messaging look like? What should our external messaging look like?
- What does our change management plan look like? How do we get our staff engaged in this plan?

As the organization answered each question, they placed a plank, building the bridge backwards from the destination point to the origin point. Answering these (and many other questions) enables leadership to see the "whole." Changes were not made in silos, they were made with the big picture in mind.

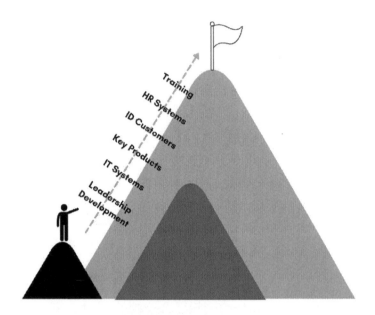

That holistic perspective allowed the organization to optimize their potential, every step of the way.

Lighting a Team Fire

COptOs can't get things done on their own. It takes a team. And it works best when the team members have very different thoughts, ideas and perspectives. The Baldrige criteria provides an expansive point of view when it comes to diversity.[33] They suggest that diversity includes race, religion, color, gender, national origin, disability, sexual orientation, age and generation, education, geographic origin, skill characteristics, ideas, thinking, academic disciplines, and perspectives.

We love the research that's out there on this topic.

Diversity is actually GOOD for an organization.

A McKinsey study found that "Companies in the top quartile for racial and ethnic diversity are 35 percent more likely to have financial returns above their respective national industry medians."[34]

A Deloitte report found that cognitively and demographically diverse teams can enhance innovation by 20% and identify/reduce risks by up to 30%.[35]

Teams with diverse perspectives are more likely to solve a problem than non-diverse teams, according to an experiment run by the Harvard Business Review.[36]

And to put the cherry on the top – diverse teams make better decisions. In fact, one study suggested that diversity can improve decision making by a whopping 60%.[37]

To tap into this diversity of thought, we suggested that this organization use something we call "Sparkshops." And if starting with the end in mind is vision and strategy, Sparkshops provide the tactics!

The entire organization – from frontline employees through the upper management – was brought together and introduced to the new strategy: "Innovative Success." Once the strategy was defined and understood, the entire group was asked to identify what could be done to achieve this goal.

Notice the phrase: "what could be."

Sparkshops are not about one right answer. They are not about "hit-it-out-of-the-park" solutions. Sparkshops follow a very formal process that gives the participants the freedom to identify, build on, prioritize, choose, refine, and implement a variety of end-in-mind methodologies that when put together as a whole, take the organization closer to their goal.

Typically, these methodologies consist of small- to medium-sized projects or opportunities that can be completed with the organization's existing resources. These ideas:
- Come from the team...
- Are prioritized by the team...
- Are planned and refined by the team...
- Are implemented by the team...
- And are completed by the team!

And that process lights a fire in the team – hence the name, Sparkshop. The first year, this organization embraced seven Sparkshop methodologies. The following year, they measured their progress and adopted another five ideas.

Today, the organization's deliberate process of starting with the end in mind, looking at holistic solutions versus departmental solutions, and inviting everyone in the organization to play has changed the trajectory of the organization.

They have an international presence. They are known for their innovative practices. And they have raised revenues to the point where they are able to donate a portion of their admissions fees to causes that are dear to the organization and the people who work there.

That's a story with a happy ending. But what happens when a holistic perspective isn't taken into consideration? Let's look at a very different story.

Imagine building a flyover bridge. It's a $23 million dollar project designed to improve the flow of traffic between two major highways. Six piers will support an exit ramp that will enable traffic to cross over one highway and merge into different highway. The money has been allocated. The plans have been drawn and approved. And the contractors have been hired.

More than a year later, the first milestone of the project has been completed and the support piers are in place. Now it's time for milestone two. Steel contractors have been brought in to install the long beams that will join the piers together and form the base of the roadbed.

But now, there is a problem. The piers are not the right height. They are several inches too tall.[38] Unfortunately, that's a true story. And it happens all the time – inside organizations. Without a holistic perspective, leaders, departments, and/or divisions make changes, only to discover that their decisions cause all sorts of grief in other areas of the organization.

You've seen it happen. You've experienced the re-work. You've witnessed the wasted excellence. And you've lived with the results of diminished team dynamics and staff morale.

What's frustrating about these types of situations is that most leaders – at least the ones we have worked with – don't mean to be myopic and silo-oriented. In fact, they have the best of intentions; however, they're too often department-focused. They know their employees' work. They understand their outputs. And they are rewarded for their department's productivity. They are NOT rewarded for seeing, understanding, and taking care of the "whole."

COptOs must have a holistic perspective so that they can define the end goal, bring the appropriate players to the table, illuminate all the connection points, build a cohesive plan, AND bring the team into alignment.

HOLISTIC PERSPECTIVE
Reinforcement Resources

Systems thinking is a discipline for seeing wholes. It is a framework for seeing inter-relationships rather than things, for seeing patterns of change rather than static snapshots.

— Peter Senge

1. Think about a project that you are working on. Start with the end in mind. What are you trying to accomplish? What does success look like? What is done? Build the plan backwards – from finish to start.
Download a Free *Build the Bridge* template, at: chiefoptimizationofficer.com/tools

2. Look at your team. Where are you already diverse? Where do you have opportunity to add diversity?

3. How are you tapping into the diversity of your team? How could you do it EVEN better?

PART II
SUCCESS METHODOLOGIES

7
FACILITATION

"No matter the organization, the goal, or the mission, you've got to do it through people."
— retired Admiral Mike Mullens

Great Chief Optimization Officers don't need to HAVE all the answers – they just need to be humble enough and curious enough to work with others to FIND answers. And the skill set we talked about in Chapter 3 was facilitation.

What IS facilitation?

We discovered that facilitation means stepping away from "being the expert to enabling others to become experts. It's the adjustment in one's thinking from believing YOU have the answers to empowering others to discover answers."

We can't tell you how many people have said: "That sounds easy enough." We truly WISH it was easy! It's not. So, let's break this skill set of facilitation down into the three A's. Airtime, Asking, and Asylum.

Airtime

What percentage of airtime do you consume? Think about your meetings, your 1:1s, your Zoom calls, your drop-ins. What percentage of that time are YOU talking – dominating the airtime?

The research on this is fascinating. A Plunkett, Tost, Gino, and Larrick study says that when formal leaders (individuals with management titles and direct reports) do the majority of the talking, team performance diminishes.[39]

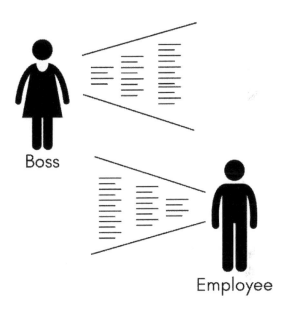

Boss

Employee

WOW! Dominating airtime has a direct negative impact on results.[40] And OUCH! Some of us are screwed!!

Those who know Tammy know she is a talker. She likes to process out loud with other people. And Tammy has thoughts and ideas that she thinks will expand the conversation and allow the team to explore it further. She also processes information very quickly.

So, it's not unusual for her to have something to share before other people have even formulated their opinions.

Even though she knows better, Tammy dominates conversations.

When leaders dominate airtime, they send a message to their team – that the team's voices, their ideas, their experience is not important. This might not be what you actually think or believe, but unfortunately, people respond to your actions – not your motives. So, what happens when you dominate conversations? Your team will stop sharing. You have taught them to wait.

Again, think about your meetings, your 1:1s, your Zoom calls, your drop-ins. How often is there silence? Not silence, as in people are thinking and/or pondering a great question. We're talking about silence that demonstrates a reluctance or unwillingness to speak up.

Timothy R. Clark in his book, The 4 Stages of Psychological Safety says that "unnatural silence is usually an indication that a team has been neutralized by its leader."[41] And we've been in boardroom after boardroom where executive leaders have asked questions, only to be greeted with silence.

When we've debriefed these meetings, we've heard many of these same executives question the intellect of their teams.

Yikes! What does THAT suggest?

Believe it or not, people ARE brilliant – if YOU allow them to be. And tracking your airtime may be one of the most eye-opening and organizational transformation exercises you could ever do.

"People ARE brilliant - if YOU allow them to be."

Think through the following questions.

- What percentage of the time are you talking?
- How often do you lead the conversation?
- Who brings answers to the table? How often is that person you?

- What happens when someone asks a question? Do you provide the answer, or do you ask another question?
- How often are you the breaker of the silence?
- Who speaks up first? How often is that person you?
- What's happening when you feel like you HAVE TO contribute?
- What happens after you contribute?
- What could you do to minimize your contribution and maximize your team's contribution?

If we were to guess, many of you will read this list, spend a moment pondering the questions, go on to the next paragraph, and never track your airtime.

That would be a mistake.

Uncovering HOW and WHEN you contribute to conversations can change everything. And we mean EVERYTHING.

Everything from:

- the effort your employees bring to the table,
- to innovative solutions,
- to staff growth and development,
- to problem solving,
- to organizational productivity,
- and even to bottom line results.

Believe it or not, the quantity of your words and the timing of your words has that much impact.

At the end of this chapter, you will find an airtime tracker. If you're a formal leader (someone with direct reports), we recommend that you use the airtime tracker to document and analyze how and when you contribute in typical situations like your weekly team meetings, 1:1s, project status meetings, and even when someone drops in with a question. If you were to track your airtime in each of these situations, you will more than likely identify places where you could slow down, be more patient, and allow others to lead the way.

And one more thing. When you decide to make space for others and stop dominating conversation, expect long awkward silences – at least for a while. If your team is used to YOU filling in the blank, they have learned to wait for you to speak. And they are VERY GOOD at waiting. You're going to have to learn to wait THEM out.

We told you this was NOT going to be easy! 😊 #NOTeasy

Asking

Scott is not great at waiting. He's a "bit" (a sarcastic statement, to say the least) impatient. And very driven. So, he is always pushing and pressing for results. As his father would say, "Don't put off to tomorrow something you can do today."

He'd like to believe that impatience is beneficial. And just like most people, he's found "proof" that aligns with this core belief. Entrepreneur Bradley Tusk, believes that impatience IS a virtue. "Impatience means setting your own course, trying as many avenues as possible to get something done, trying out new ideas, new approaches, [and] new intellectual frameworks to increase your odds of making something happen."[42]
All good things...until you need to get things done with and through other people. Then impatience bites you in the A$$.

When you are the driver and don't make room for others to contribute, YOU will always be in charge. YOU become the over-achiever who enables others to under-achieve. YOU will end up being the smartest person in the room. And the answers, the results that your team will achieve, will be limited to what YOU can bring to the table.

Maybe that sounds good to you. For us, that's scary. Scott is smart and capable, AND, he does not have all the answers. And while he might be observant and empathetic, he doesn't fully understand what it is like to walk in other's shoes...NONE of us do.

So, if you are not all-knowing and powerful, maybe there are other people whose experience, education, understanding and/or perspectives would add value to the conversation. And if that's true, then asking powerful questions can tap into their knowledge and unique gifts.

Just in case we haven't made it clear, COptOs are not lone wolves who level up an organization based upon their own intellect and effort. That's the story of Paul in Chapter 1. Nor are Chief Optimization Officers responsible for one-and-done change management efforts. Leveling up is a continuous and iterative process.

"Leveling up is a continuous and iterative process."

It requires the talent, intellect, and effort of every individual inside an organization. And successful Chief Optimization Officers build the structures, the processes, and the environments that enable individuals – in every role across the organization – to participate in the leveling-up process. To do that, every employee needs to be able to think things through and contribute in meaningful ways. That's why COptOs need to ask powerful questions.

Powerful questions:

- Are open-ended
- Can be used in any situation – without editing
- And some powerful questions are not questions at all

We often challenge leaders to develop a list of twenty powerful questions in 10 minutes or less. So, if you'd like to take the challenge – stop reading, close the book, set a timer for 10 minutes and write down your list of powerful questions – as quickly as you can.

If you'd rather take the easy road, see our list on the next page.

Twenty Powerful Questions

1. Tell me more about that...
2. Help me understand. Walk me through your thinking.
3. What have we done in the past? What else is possible?
4. If you were to make the decision, what would you decide to do, and why?
5. Play that out for me. What do you think will happen?
6. What are you/we trying to accomplish?
7. Walk me through the data story.
8. What outcome(s) are you hoping for?
9. What options and/or alternatives did you consider? Why did you choose this option?
10. What are the advantages (strengths, benefits, upside)? What are the disadvantages (weaknesses, downside)?
11. What obstacles might get in the way? How could you overcome them?
12. What concerns might other people have? How could you address these concerns?
13. What teams/departments would see it this way? Why?
14. Who might see it differently? What's their perspective? How is their perspective valid?
15. What contrary evidence did you find? How did you address/work through that/those perspective(s)?
16. Who else needs to get involved? What could their involvement look like? How will that help you achieve your goal/outcome?
17. What else?
18. And...
19. What does your plan look like? How will you go about that? What's next?
20. What worked? What didn't work? What would you do differently next time?

Do you need to memorize all these questions? No. It is helpful, however, to have a set of questions that rolls off your tongue easily and will help you engage others in the process of thinking, considering, and suggesting. We have our favorites.

What powerful questions are going to be YOUR favorites?

Scott's Powerful Questions	Tammy's Powerful Questions
What does good look like?	Tell me more...
Who is "they"?	What else?
What's the impact of that?	What's right about that?
Let's go look...	What obstacles do you see?
What have you found so far?	How could we overcome them?

Your Powerful Questions

Now comes the hard part.

- You KNOW you need to be an asker instead of a teller.

- You're ARMED with a set of powerful questions that you can ask anytime, anywhere.

- You SEE an opportunity to ask a question. AND now you have to:

**Ask,
Shut Up, and
Wait for It**

Again, we told you this was NOT going to be easy! #REALLYNOTEASY

Asylum

Historically, organizational safety has focused on physical safety. The Occupational and Safety Health Act passed by Congress in 1970 was put in place to protect workers from safety and health hazards, such as exposure to toxic chemicals, excessive noise levels, mechanical dangers, heat or cold stress, or unsanitary conditions.[43] More than fifty years later – there is little doubt that OSHA regulations have saved hundreds of thousands of lives and prevented millions of injuries.

That's a good thing, but physical safety is not the only safety classification to consider. Organizations must also understand the effects of psychological safety.

In her best-selling book *Smart Tribes*, Christine Comaford said, "Human brains are wired to seek safety, belonging, and mattering. Many scientific management practices from the Industrial Age, as well as our own unconscious safety patterning, can inadvertently push our people into acting out of fear, crush our culture, and stifle innovation and growth."[44]

That's why we love the word asylum.

What is asylum? It is defined as "*an inviolable place of refuge and safety.*" And we know that COptOs need to create asylum, a place of psychological safety, if they want people to truly contribute.

> "COptOs need to create asylum, a place of psychological safety, if they want people to truly contribute."

In our workshop, Extreme Facilitation, we have used a tool called Five Levels of Self-Disclosure, for almost 30 years. The premise is that it is the facilitator's role to create asylum in the classroom and it is a step-by-step process.

When you intentionally take action to walk with individuals up each step, you are creating asylum. And each step along the way strengthens the relationship and creates a deeper sense of safety, belonging, and mattering.

5 Levels of Self-Disclosure

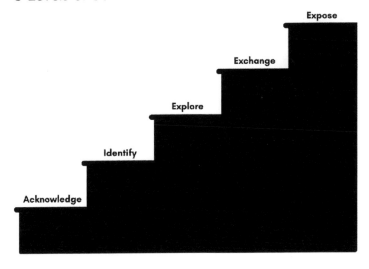

Level 1: Acknowledge

The first level of disclosure is relatively easy and comfortable. We all have standard ways of acknowledging other human beings. In rural Iowa, we have the one-finger wave. When two vehicles pass one another on a rural road going in opposite directions, the standard procedure is to raise your right-hand index finger to essentially say hello. The same thing happens in office hallways every day when people make eye contact, nod their head in acknowledgement or say, "good morning."

This act of acknowledgement is critical to asylum. It says, "I see you AND you are worth my time and effort."

For many years, Tammy and her husband, along with her parents, had a side-gig selling antique glass and porcelain at shows throughout the Midwest. They were often teased about the number of people in their booth and how loud they were. Tammy always believed that was because they started every relationship with acknowledgement.

Most of their peer vendors simply sat in their booths and waited for customers to start the conversation. They would bide their time reading books, cruising the Internet for inventory, or talking with other vendors. And the only time they acknowledged a new customer was when the customer asked them a question.

In comparison, Tammy's crew made eye contact. They smiled. They said hello. And Tammy often joked with people as they walked by. Sure, some people ignored them or ducked and ran. However, a fair amount of people acknowledged them back. After 20 years Tammy and her family retired the business. And at their last show, over 1,000 people from around the country purposely drove to a small town of 5,500 in Northwest Iowa to say goodbye.

Without acknowledgement, relationships don't have the opportunity to develop. And when people withhold acknowledgement – whether purposefully or not – relationships are damaged.

Consider the manager who is often deep in thought as he walks through the atrium each afternoon and doesn't say hello to members of his team. Or the employee who chronically runs behind every morning, so she rushes through the building to reach her desk by 8 am. More than likely, neither of these individuals purposefully ignored their teammates.

You've probably been at the receiving end of this kind of unintended thoughtlessness. It doesn't feel good. It doesn't make you feel safe. It doesn't encourage you to interact with this individual. And it doesn't lay the groundwork for a more meaningful relationship.

Level 2: Identify

The second level of self-disclosure is Identify. In our workshops we often begin the day with introductions. We ask people to tell us a little bit about themselves – both personally and professionally.

Often, we'll hear something like:

> *Hi. My name is Tammy Rogers. I work at Aveea Partners, an organizational and leadership development firm. Aveea is located in West Des Moines, Iowa and has been around for 27 years. I'm originally from the Chicago area. I moved to Iowa in 1984. I'm married. I met Michael playing volleyball 30 years ago. We don't have kids. We do, however, have two fur babies.*

This ritual plays out in corporate America daily. And most of us see this level of disclosure as harmless so long as people follow the "unofficial" rules:

- Be friendly.
- Don't brag.
- Share things that are sociably acceptable in this setting.
- Don't make it awkward.
- Don't get too intimate.

When we're at this level, most of the time it doesn't feel scary. That's because we are sharing "surface facts." The information is personal, but not personal enough that if someone judged it or teased us about it, it would hurt our feelings. In fact, we often share this kind of information to help us discover what we have in common with other people. Think about it.

How many times have you started a conversation with someone simply because you found that you both lived in the same community, or had kids in the same school, or enjoyed the same kind of activity? We choose to reveal safe information about ourselves in Level 2 to help us connect with other human beings.

Occasionally we have seen an issue with safety at Level 2. We call it the "one-up game". You've probably seen it. One person announces that they have an MBA. And then the next person "one-ups" them by sharing they have a PhD. Or someone shares that they have six direct reports, and another individual "one-ups" them by sharing that they have fifteen direct reports.

One of Scott's most memorable "one-ups" happened when a group was discussing their favorite places to travel. One after another, individuals shared stories about Yellowstone Park, the Outer Banks of South Carolina, and New York City. The group then turned to the last member of their team and asked him about his favorite place to travel and he asked: "On what continent?"

That's not asylum. That's ego! And ego kills psychological safety.

Level 3: Explore

We like to think about level three this way. It's a hot day. The sun is shining. And the lake looks inviting, but, before anyone commits, they need to test the water by dipping their toes in first.

Come on, admit it. You've done this. Sometimes it's just too daunting to jump in. So, you feel things out to see what happens.

In Extreme Facilitation, we purposefully push people from Identify into Explore. It happens after the first participant facilitates their session and everyone is required to provide both positive and negative feedback. We start by having each participant share something they thought went well.

The first time out, people will say things like:

- Good tone, great pace.
- Seemed comfortable.
- Looks like you were really prepared.

Then, when asked to provide constructive feedback, the participants often say things like:

- It was all good. IF I HAD to say something, I would say you might need a little more confidence.
- You really did a good job. Just one small thing: your PowerPoint slides were a little busy.
- Gosh, I really can't think of anything else. You did a REALLY good job.

Talk about vanilla! That's a lot of people, not saying much of anything. And that's what we do when we're in level three. We're careful. We know we need to step things up. We know we're expected to share. We know that this is the time to show folks what we've got. And we're feeling very vulnerable. So, we explore the boundaries by expressing "basic" ideas and judgments. We share "safe" opinions. We divulge "innocuous" information. And we provide "anemic" analysis.

Most of us probably have much stronger opinions than what we expressed. However, at this point we've hedged our bets. We were only courageous enough to push the boundary a little bit. And now we're watching and waiting. We're trying to decipher where the boundary is. And we won't share any more of ourselves if our vanilla, basic, safe, innocuous, and anemic responses are not well received.

If employees test the water – only to find that it's just too uncomfortable for them to jump in – they stay on the shoreline. And then find very creative ways to appear like they are contributing – without having to really get wet.

And that's a shame!

Remember the Midwest Nice concept that we shared in Chapter 2? Sometimes we keep opinions to ourselves so not to offend others. And sometimes we keep opinions to ourselves because it's doesn't feel safe to share.

You might remember that we said we purposefully pushed Extreme Facilitation participants into Explore. Why? Psychological safety doesn't just happen. It requires asylum. And asylum can only be achieved as people progress through the levels of self-disclosure. Explore is simply ONE step along the way. The key is to validate the individual's contributions, even if the contributions are vanilla, basic, safe, innocuous, and anemic.

Acceptance at this juncture is mandatory if you want people to participate in a deeper and more meaningful way in the future. If people feel safe when they test the water, eventually they will take a chance and step up to Level 4: Exchange.

Level 4: Exchange

The first three levels of self-disclosure are basically mandatory. Most organizations demand acknowledgement – think inclusion. Most organizations require a minimum amount of personal disclosure – consider that emotional intelligence is often more highly valued than cognitive intelligence. And most organizations expect some amount of exploration. Honestly, could you imagine what might happen if an employee always refused to participate or contribute to a conversation?

Basically, employees HAVE TO make it to Level 3. Level 4? Well, that's another story. And this is where discretionary effort comes in.

According to Mike Zani, the CEO of Predictive Index and the author of the best-selling book, The Science of Dream Teams, discretionary effort is the difference between "have to" and "want to."[45]

What do I have to do to keep my job? I have to show up for work. I have to get along with my co-workers. I have to complete my assignments on time. Well, most of my assignments. Well, assignments that I don't have a good excuse for not getting them done on time. 😄

We use the phrase minimum expectations to describe these requirements. Minimum expectations are the actions, attitudes, and behaviors that an employee HAS TO demonstrate to remain employed, and at many organizations, this bar is set extremely low.

Consider the organization that DOES NOT:

- Require drug testing... because the majority of the staff wouldn't pass.
- Expect fulltime staff to show up to work five days a week... because a good portion of the workforce doesn't make it to work on Mondays and/or Fridays.
- Don't hold salespeople to organizational procedures and behavioral standards... simply because they refuse to comply.
- Allow people to miss deadline after deadline... without saying a word.

Successful organizations SET minimum expectations. However, they are not SATISFIED if their staff only meets these minimums. They know that each member of their team has more to offer. And they recognize that it is the organization's responsibility to create an environment where employees WANT TO bring this discretionary effort to the table.

Now, here's what is interesting.

Permissiveness is NOT what encourages people to bring their discretionary effort. We're not talking about coddling people or creating a get-along culture. We're talking about giving people's thoughts, ideas, and opinions a hearing. When leaders themselves are non-reactive, when they slow down, listen to and consider other people's perspectives AND set standards for the entire team to slow down, be non-reactive, listen to and consider other people's perspectives, they create a safe zone that allows people to step up to Level 4.

You see, as the stakes have been raised, the staff has been watching and waiting. They have tested the organization's tolerance for feedback and dissent. They have checked to ensure that they will not be unfairly judged or ridiculed. They have decided if their team has their back. And they have determined if their leader will support them – even as they learn new things and make mistakes – even when they have bad days. You see, no one will stick their neck out if it's going to be chopped off.

"No one will stick their neck out if it's going to be chopped off."

If their analysis assures them that the environment is safe, then the employee is willing to step up to Level 4. They will share their ideas, disagree, explore options and alternatives, fight for the best solutions, and align with decisions. And they will bring this discretionary effort to the table because they feel safe. Their leader has created asylum.

Level 4 is the goal, and the only way to reach it is to start at Level 1 and walk up the steps together. And at each step there is a decision point. Does it feel safe enough for me to expose more of myself? If the answer is yes, when the next opportunity comes, they may take that next leap of faith and go up a level. And they may not.

Every employee brings history with them and their past experiences are going to form the basis for their decision. If they have been burned in the past, getting to Level 4 may take a while. They are going to need to see consistent and on-going evidence that it's truly different here. They will need to experience that their leader is not going to punish them if they:

- Are learning and make mistakes.
- See things differently and have a differing opinion.
- Sometimes don't use the right words or tone to get their message across.
- Challenge the status quo.

AND they will need to see consistent and on-going evidence that they are a member of the tribe. Their team is FOR them, not against them. They belong and are a needed and necessary member of the team.

Of course, YOU will screw up. TEAM MEMBERS will screw up.

When that happens, you will end up taking two steps backward and will need to re-build the trust. And that's just part of this never-ending journey to create asylum.

Yep. We told you this was NOT going to be easy! 😊   #NOTF@%$ingeasy

Level 5: Expose

Yes. There ARE five levels of self-disclosure. And we've only discussed four.

People typically reserve Level 5 for their most intimate relationships: spouses, the closest of friends – and if you happen to work in a very intimate organization – maybe a business partner.

You'll recognize Level 5 because it's a place where people can bring their loftiest hopes and their darkest fears. It's a place where people can belly laugh until they wet their pants. It's a place where people can get really angry and ugly cry. It happens when there is no veneer between two people. It's the safe haven where you are truly known, loved, and accepted, in spite of all of your warts.

Level 5 probably won't happen at work.

FACILITATION

Reinforcement Resources

"Without a good question, a good answer has no place to go."
– Clayton Christensen

1. Airtime Tracker
    - Identify your recurring meetings.
    - Track your airtime in comparison to the rest of the attendees at each meeting. When a question is asked, note who answered it.
    - What did you notice or learn? What do you need to do differently?

2. Identifying the types of questions you ask will help you determine how to improve participation, innovation, and engagement – question types: chiefoptimizationofficer.com/tools

3. Creating asylum is critical to boost discretionary effort. Take our asylum assessment to understand how your behavior impacts asylum: chiefoptimizationofficer.com/tools

8
SIMPLIFY

"Making the simple complicated is commonplace; making the complicated simple, awesomely simple, that's creativity."

— Charles Mingus

Complexity Bias

Have you ever been impressed by complexity? We have.

Years ago, a start-up that Tammy worked with created a spreadsheet that told the story of their operations plan. It was beautiful. If you wanted to know how many employees they were going to need and by when – the answer was in the spreadsheet. If you wanted to understand transportation costs – it was in the spreadsheet. And if you wanted to decide what was the best way to modify the burn rate – you could play with the data in the spreadsheet.

At that time, Excel was REALLY new, so Tammy was truly in awe. When she had questions – the CEO opened the spreadsheet and showed Tammy the answer. When the investors had questions, the CEO walked them through the spreadsheet. And when you there were cashflow issues – well, you get it – it was in the spreadsheet.

The CEO had spent months developing the spreadsheet, and it tracked everything. Budgets were in the spreadsheet. Trainees' efficiency rates were in the spreadsheet. Even the sales staff hit ratios were in the spreadsheet.

Tammy never questioned the spreadsheet. And neither did anyone else.

Why? Because of something called "complexity bias." Complexity bias is the belief that complex solutions are better than simple ones. And we all suffer from it. Consider the individual who is experiencing recurring headaches and thinks it's a brain tumor. Or the salesperson who spends hours analyzing and then justifying why they are not hitting their sales goals when they haven't picked up the phone in a week to call potential customers.

Complexity bias is a standard neurological hack, a cognitive shortcut, much like the I'm right bias we talked about in Chapter 3. The I'm right or knowledge bias speeds things up because it encourages us to choose the option we already know and understand. Confirmation bias keeps us from spending time updating our beliefs. The availability bias is a timesaver because it allows us to avoid thinking through and considering everything we know about a topic. How is the complexity bias a neurological hack? When we label something "complex" we abdicate our responsibility to understand it. We don't take the time to learn or understand it. And we end up giving our power to the individual who "understands" and "controls" the complexity.

Let us give you a couple of examples.

Jargon. How many times have you interacted with someone who used big words, obscure terminology, or acronyms that were unfamiliar to you? They didn't explain what these terms meant, and you never asked. Did you assume they were smart?

Math. Have you ever been handed a balance sheet and assumed that someone else knew how to read it and would ensure that the numbers were accurate?

Technology. Can you think of a time where you let someone else handle the technology instead of mastering it yourself?

Marketers and salespeople have been known to purposefully use complexity bias to their advantage. Complexity is also used as a negotiation tactic. And sometimes, true experts don't take the time to make things simple and inject complexity into the system and/or organization without intending to.

What's the result? Complexity kills understanding, initiative, productivity, progress, profitability, growth, and even personal and organizational success. In fact, a joint Bain and Economist Intelligence Unit survey found that 85% of CEOs from failed organizations blamed complexity for their downfall.[46]

> "Complexity kills understanding, initiative, productivity, progress, profitability, growth, and even personal and organizational success."

We've witnessed continuous improvement efforts that led to increased organizational complexity. That is why COptOs focus on ensuring that solutions are simple.

Seven Methods of Simplifying

Simplicity doesn't just happen. It takes a conscious and deliberate effort. Let us introduce you to seven methods that you can use to simplify – well, just about everything.

- Start with the End in Mind.
- Identify Connections.
- Define the Minimum Viable Product.
- Embrace the Power of Delete.
- Create Constructive Constraints.
- Along the Way Ask: Is this Essential?.
- Practice Explaining it to your 5th Grader.

Start with the End in Mind

Yes, we talked about this in Chapter 6 – and it bears repeating. Why? In our experience – very few people take the time to decide what "done" looks like. They jump in and start doing without taking the time to think. For many of us, doing – taking action – is more comfortable than thinking.

We see this in workshop after workshop. We give participants a task. We provide them with planning time. But they seldom use it. The group typically just jumps in and starts running.

We shouldn't be surprised. A study conducted by Timothy Wilson, a social psychologist at the University of Virginia, found that when people were left on their own to think – for as little as 15 minutes – 67% of men and 25% of women decided to jolt themselves with an electric shock versus just sitting there and thinking.[47]

What!?!?

That research cracks us up! And it proves the point.

Many of us embrace action over planning. And if you're thinking that's not you...have you ever been stuck in traffic and gotten off at an exit, simply because moving forward, driving somewhere – anywhere – was better than sitting in traffic? Busted!

Now, don't misunderstand our message. We're all in for Dan Ward's concept of Fast, Inexpensive, Restrained, and Elegant (FIRE).[48] We like the idea of lighting a fire under a person or a project to get it moving. However, we don't want to jump into the fire BEFORE we have clarity on what we are trying to accomplish, and agreement on where the finish line is. Clarity helps us plan, allocate resources, and decide along the way what to say yes AND no to. And if you don't start with the end in mind, you're going to experience a lot of unnecessary complexity AND complications.

Identify Connections

You have likely heard the song by The James Weldon Johnson called "Dry Bones". You might know it.

It goes like this:

> *"The foot bone connected to the leg bone,*
> *The leg bone connected to the knee bone,*
> *The knee bone connected to the thigh bone,*
> *The thigh bone connected to the backbone,*
> *The backbone connected to the neck bone,*
> *The neck bone connected to the head bone,*
> *I hear the word of the Lord"*[49]

Well, we might all need to heed the word of the Lord, because if we don't identify how things are connected inside of the organization, it's going to get messy...very soon!

The simple act of proactively identifying organizational connections allows you to get the right people at the table, reduce rework, and improve efficiencies. And it can be done with one simple tool: a process map. We could overcomplicate it. But why?

Define the Minimum Viable Product

The concept of Minimum Viable Product was introduced by Eric Ries in his book Lean Startup. Ries makes the case that you should create a simple version of your product or service and allow the customer to interact with it. Seeing how people actually use something provides much more reliable information than asking people what they want. When you ask people what they WANT, it leads to unnecessary complexity.[50] We'll say it this way. Success is:

- Not about what you *want*.
- Not about what the team *wants*.
- Not about what the C-suite *wants*.
- Not always about what the customer *wants*.

It is about what is *needed and necessary* to achieve results.

Think about the word essential. Ask yourself what HAS TO be there? More is NOT necessarily better. Additional features do not make something better. Supplementary choices do not make something more desirable. Even more innovation is not necessarily better. The simplest and easiest solution that delivers the required results is better.

That's what the words "minimum" and "viable" mean. Your solution must work, AND it should not include anything above and beyond what is needed and necessary to get the desired results.

Embrace the Power of Delete

Sometimes our ideas, features, and innovations go beyond our agreed upon minimum viable product. When that happens, the question we are always asked is: "Now that we have these features, should we leave them out?" The answer is YES. If the feature is redundant, unnecessary, unwanted, unneeded (and did we say redundant?), then yes, it needs to be eliminated.

Wow. That sounds serious. And final. And maybe a bit scary. Yes AND, holding on to things that don't move us forward end up as dead weight. Carrying around dead weight is exhausting.

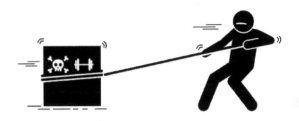

Embracing the power of delete is liberating. Just think about it for a minute.

Embrace the Power of Delete	
Keeping Things Requires	**Deleting Things Provides**
• Additional Tracking	• More Time
• Extra Organization	• Simplified Decision-making
• Superfluous Thinking	• Increased Focus
• Increased Distractions	• Fewer Distractions

P.S.: That's why our book is short, sweet, and to the point!

#DeletingisFun

Create Constructive Constraints

Ever heard of Parkinson's Law? It stems from an essay written by C. Northcote Parkinson who said, "It is a commonplace observation that work expands so as to fill the time available for its completion."[51]

Isn't that the truth? Somehow, every one of Scott's college papers took exactly the number of hours he had from the time he started them to the time he turned them in. Amazing!

And here's how you turn a negative into a positive...

There's an upside to procrastination. When you create constructive constraints, it forces you into simplicity. You don't have time for anything other than creating a minimum viable product.

Now, we are not actually suggesting that you procrastinate. We are however, suggesting that you use time gates.

Time gates put a limit on the number of hours you allow yourself to complete a task. You could set a time gate for writing an email, chatting with a co-worker, or configuring a new software system. Tammy actually had a business partner who put a time gate on the number of hours she allowed herself to mope! That's impressive!

We have found that time gates not only build a culture of simplicity, they also help us:

- Prioritize.
- Let go of Perfectionism.
- Speed Up Decision-Making.
- Get More Done.

Along the Way Ask: Is this Essential?

Another one of Dan Ward's models is The Simplicity Cycle. His model makes a great point. Not ALL complexity is bad. In fact, complexity done right is often a differentiator. It can make us money. However, if overdone, it can cost us time and money. That's why we need to stop occasionally and ask if what we are doing is essential.[52]

We've modified Ward's model to point out a critical decision point.

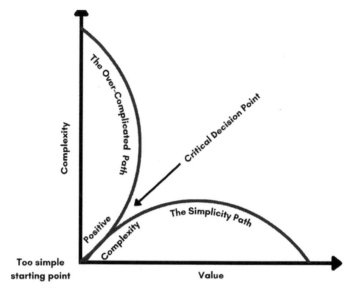

Adapted from Dan Ward's Simplicity Cycle Model

There comes a time in every project when complexity is no longer good. That's why we need to stop occasionally to ask if what we are doing is essential. If it is – then you are still on the positive complexity slope where good and complexity are aligned. If the answer is no, then the wise decision is to take a right turn and head down the simplicity path. And when you actually reach this juncture and decide to take the simplicity path – you are ready to begin the editing and deleting process – which according to software guru Eric Raymond, can eventually lead to perfection "when there is nothing more to take away."[53]

Practice Explaining it to your 5th Grader

Our final method of simplifying is really about simplifying your messaging. We've all sat in too many meetings listening to someone explain a strategy, a software issue, a customer request, or an implementation plan that went completely over the audience's head. We are pretty sure these presentations made perfect sense to them, but it was gobbledygook to the rest of us.

It could have been because:

- The speaker was not organized.
- The presenter was not prepared.
- Whatever they were talking about was overly complicated.

We have always loved the game show that Jeff Foxworthy hosted, "Are You Smarter Than a Fifth Grader?" During each show, adult contestants were asked questions that were lifted straight out of elementary school textbooks. There were two questions from each grade, starting with first grade and progressing to fifth grade. And if, or should we say when, the contestant ran into trouble they could get help from – of course – real, live 5th graders.

There have only been two contestants who have won the million-dollar prize. So, if you can't explain it to a fifth grader – your message, service and/or product isn't simple enough.

"If you can't explain it to a fifth grader – your message, service and/or product isn't simple enough."

SIMPLIFY
Reinforcement Resources

"The ability to simplify means to eliminate the unnecessary so that the necessary may speak."
— Hans Hofmann

1. More than likely, you have something that you need to simplify. Get a simplification worksheet at: chiefoptimizationofficer.com/tools

2. What dead weight are you carrying? What's the impact?

3. What feedback have you heard about your messages? How could you ensure that even a 5th grader would understand what you are saying?

9
INCREMENTAL GROWTH

"Without continual growth and progress, such words as improvement, achievement, and success have no meaning."

– Benjamin Franklin

The big win. We all dream about it. Baseball players dream about grand slam homeruns. Musicians dream about a Billboard #1 hit. And actors dream about winning an Academy Award.

Big wins make headlines. They are memorable. They make us feel successful. And they encourage us to swing for the fence.

But BIG is not the only way to win. Consider this: some millionaires got there by buying a lottery ticket. Most millionaires, however, accumulated their wealth by working long and hard hours over the course of twenty or more years. They don't have one big win. They have consistent and incremental wins.

The same principle applies to organizations. There is a ton of buzz when a company wins big. Pop culture would suggest that Amazon is an example of a big winner. Yet when you review Amazon's timeline, it lays out a very different story.[54]

A snapshot of Amazon's history

1998: Adds products: music, DVD's,
software and video games

1994: Amazon Founded   1999: Adds one click buying

2002: Adds Amazon Web
Services (back-end provider
for organizations like Netflix).

2005: Adds Amazon Prime

2000: Allows third-party merchants

Notice that Amazon did not win with a single idea, product, or service. They won in their first 10 years of existence by making incremental changes. And while Amazon may have done it better than many organizations, they are not the only organization that believes in incremental growth. According to Entrepreneur Magazine, 98% of all organizational innovations are incremental.[55]

So, what does incremental growth really mean? It's really about growing an organization by focusing resources on making improvements to existing products, services, processes, and/or tools.

Believe it or not, the Apple iPhone is a great example. In 2007, the iPhone was a radically new innovation. At the time, it totally changed the look, feel, and capabilities of cellular phones. However, Apple swiftly moved from a radical innovation strategy to an incremental growth strategy for the iPhone. In the fourteen years since its introduction, there have been 13 different iPhone series. And as of the fall of 2021, Apple has released a total of 33 unique iPhone models. Each phone has represented incremental growth. More storage. A better camera. Increased connectivity. A longer battery life. Wireless AirPods.

So why would a company – especially one that has been known for big wins – choose incremental growth? There are a lot of reasons.

Reduced Risk

According to Harvard Business School professor Clayton Christensen, each year more than 30,000 new consumer products are launched. And 95% of them fail.[56]

To add a little fuel to the fire, it typically costs a company about $15 million dollars to launch a new product.[57] Ouch! We don't spend a lot of time in Vegas, but we believe that means when an organization relies on a radical or a disruptive growth strategy, they are actually making a bet with a 5% chance of winning. Of course, if you've got a big bank account, $15 million might be chump-change. If, however, you are a small or medium sized U.S. business -- $15 million might mean you are placing an all-or-nothing bet.

Incremental growth strategies allow organizations of all sizes to make a series of small bets, on a variety of ideas, innovations, and improvements, without putting the company in harm's way.

Voice of the Customer

Contrary to popular belief, Apple really does listen to the voice of the customer – in a very purposeful and systematic way.[58] You can trace it back to Steve Jobs in 1997 when he said, "*you've got to start with the customer experience and work backwards to the technology.*"

Since then, Apple continues to use a variety of customer feedback methodologies – including, believe it or not, market research to listen to the voice of the customer. They email surveys to customers immediately after a purchase is made. They faithfully gather, analyze, and monitor Net Promotor Scores. And they use good-old-fashioned feedback surveys to ask questions like, "What else is on your mind?"

The result? Apple dominates the American Customer Satisfaction Index – with iPhone, Mac, and iPad rated #1 in their respective categories.[59] What does this have to do with incremental growth? Apple has been able to use voice of the customer data to create repeat buyers.

According to a recent SellCell survey, 92% of iPhone users will stick with Apple when it comes time to upgrade.[60]

That's one heck of a statistic, especially when you consider that the average customer retention rate for major U.S. industries falls somewhere between 63% - 84%.[61]

Retention Rate by Industry	
63%	Retail
75%	Banking
78%	Telecom
81%	IT
83%	Insurance
84%	Professional Services
84%	Media

Apple's repeat buyers will purchase products that were designed and released with an incremental growth mindset. And when these repeat customers receive those products – they will find the next best thing – which is exactly what they told Apple they wanted!

Improve Competitiveness

Incremental growth enables an organization to generate profits from a current product WHILE they are developing the next iteration. That cash flow provides the organization with the time and stability to radically innovate if they so desire. And it helps the organization keep their current customers close, retain market share, and stay top-of-mind. That improves the organization's competitiveness.

Incremental growth also enables organizations to take steps to improve their internal processes and tools. Think process improvement, automation, and The DMAIC Way® events.

We just completed a DMAIC Way® project for a small Midwest manufacturer. A simple process map along with a time study uncovered an opportunity to save the organization 2,900 hours a year. This one simple change will increase their production rate by 12%. And considering that they have a huge backlog, we're pretty sure this incremental change will help them be more competitive!

Sexy

You may not think incremental growth is sexy. We do! That's why we used Apple and Amazon as our examples. Both these organizations would be in the running for the "sexiest company alive" right now. And both companies have benefited from incremental growth.

And what about that small Midwest manufacturer? Well, if you walked their production floor, you might not notice anything extraordinary. There's no fancy equipment or automation. They don't have a state-of-the-art facility. We wouldn't suggest that this organization looks different from any small-town, home-grown manufacturing company. It's really a pretty normal place. What's not normal is achieving a 12% production increase by making one small incremental change, especially when you recognize that this is just one change of many, all of which will positively impact the organization's bottom line – this year! Their focus and commitment to incremental growth has made them pretty attractive. They are attracting new customers, additional talent, better terms, and even a buyer or two. We think that is REALLY sexy!

So, we've shared with you what incremental growth is and why it makes sense. Now let's look at some incremental growth best practices.

Incremental Growth Best Practice #1: Look for Love

You might not know the song lyrics "looking for love in all of the wrong places," but that's what people often do. They start with one person's pet project or pet peeve. And those are the wrong places.

You are better off looking at areas in your organization where there is an opportunity for a visible return on investment. A place where you can measure the difference, and a place where the difference will have a significant impact. Where are some of the more fruitful places to look for love?

Wasted Excellence: This is one of our favorite phrases. People, teams, leaders, and even organizations waste their time, expertise, and resources on things that do not add value.

Here's an example. We had a client who needed to have branded classroom materials in another city. Procurement bought the materials and had them sent to the administrative assistant. The administrative assistant received the materials, put on the appropriate brand stickers, re-packed the materials, and sent them to the training site. Oh, but wait – the workshop was in two days. So, the box needed to be sent overnight. $400 later...

Where is the waste? The $400 is obvious. And – that's not all. Funny thing – they could have just sent the materials directly to the trainer and had him put on the stickers. He was already traveling to the other city for the workshop. And he could have just paid for another bag.

That's:
- $40 bucks instead of $400
- Two sets of hands instead of three
- One shipment instead of two

Oh, and we won't tell you about the hassle when the box didn't arrive on time.

Waste is a big deal – whether you are talking about physical waste, production defects, over-production, wasted time, wasted inventory, transportation waste, or even wasted energy. Looking for incremental growth in this area often yields big returns.

Service improvements: Your customer's experience with your website, user interfaces, on-time delivery, and even product instructions have a direct impact on an organization's success. Many organizations collect and analyze customer satisfaction data to reduce customer complaints. To level up, focus on the customer experience and what the customer NEEDS (not wants) to increase your Net Promoter Scores.

Process automation: It is amazing the amount of time employees spend on repetitive tasks that could be automated. If you are like most organizations, you have both big and small processes and methodologies that would be candidates for automation, everything from spreadsheets to robotics.

Let's look at a very small example. In the last 60 days Scott shared a simple technique with our staff that automatically deletes unwanted email.

That hack (process automation) saves 15 minutes a day for each one of our employees. That might not sound like it's worth your time. If you do the math however, for the employees at our company, this one hack saves us a total of 14 days a year! And, that number doesn't even account for all the added frustration and stress that happens when you have an overflowing email box!

How many employees do YOU have?

15 minutes a day x 250 working days a year x # of employees = _____ minutes saved.

Now, imagine identifying something even more time consuming....

Incremental Growth Best Practice #2: Progress Over Perfection

We are fans of the saying "Progress over Perfection." You see, we've watched too many people and too many organizations sit and spin because they wanted the perfect answer, the perfect candidate, the perfect solution. And they were unwilling to move forward until their ideal of perfection could be realized.

We both love the True North concept from Steven Spielberg's movie Lincoln. In the movie, Thaddeus Stevens, a Radical Republican and staunch abolitionist, admonishes the president for not upholding his ideal of the "perfect" solution to the issue of slavery.

Lincoln responds by saying, "A compass, I learnt when I was surveying, it'll point you True North from where you are standing, but it's got no advice about the swamps and deserts and chasms you'll encounter along the way. If in pursuit of your destination you plunge ahead, heedless of obstacles, and achieve nothing more than to sink in a swamp, what's the use of knowing True North?"[62]

Heading towards True North makes sense. It aligns with our idea of start with the end in mind from Chapter 6. Unfortunately, you may not be able to take the most direct and perfect route. There will be swamps along the way. There will be rivers and chasms that will force you to retrace your steps. And you may have to circle around dangerous territory.

If you are stuck on perfection, you may never reach your destination. On the other hand, if you are willing to take a few steps toward True North, re-assess and then begin your next leg of the journey, you may actually arrive at True North quicker than you ever thought possible.

"If perfection is your goal, you may never reach your destination."

Incremental Growth Best Practice #3: Quick, Quick

In Chapter 5, we talked about micro and macro decisions. Macro decisions are big. They are one-way streets and once you've made a macro decision you can't take it back. For instance, once you have decided how to distribute equity and signed all the paperwork, there is no do-over. Micro decisions may also be big; however, they are reversible. You can price a product today and change the pricing model next month after you have seen how customers have responded.

- Macro decisions need to be made slow, slow.
- Micro decisions need to be made quick, quick.

Incremental growth does not require macro decision-making. Incremental growth is a small bet. It is reversible. And it is a micro decision. That means it is always quick, quick. If fact, Jeff Bezos suggests that you should make decisions with 70% of the information you wish you had. "If you wait for 90%, in most cases, you're probably being slow."[63]

There is place in most organizations for radical and disruptive growth. However, that is not the purview or responsibility of a Chief Optimization Officer. COptOs are the quiet heroes that drive incremental growth that allows the organization to continue to level up.

INCREMENTAL GROWTH
Reinforcement Resources
"Consistent, incremental development, leads to expediential growth."
— Richard Riche

1. Where do you have incremental growth opportunities?

2. Don't think you have wasted excellence? Track your meetings. If you **individually** do not bring unique value to a meeting, you don't need to attend. If you do attend – THAT is wasted excellence. Looking at your meetings last week. How much wasted excellence did you have?

3. Want to understand how you make decisions? We have an assessment for you. chiefoptimizationofficer.com/tools

10
OPTIMIZATION BURSTS

"If everything seems under control, you're not going fast enough."

— Mario Andretti

What is an optimization burst? Much like a sprint in agile software development, an optimization burst is a specific amount of time, set aside, to accomplish something of value for your customer.

There are five key elements in this definition:

Specific amount of time. Optimization bursts are not "set" intervals. You can have a four-hour, four-day, or even a four-week optimization burst.

Set aside. The length of the optimization burst may vary. What's significant is that this time is secured and reserved, and these chunks of time may not be used for any other purpose.

Accomplish something. You are not setting this time aside in case something comes up. You are not setting this time aside to catch up. You are not setting this time aside to unwind and relax. You are setting this time aside to complete a specific task.

Value. Value is difficult to identify and measure on its own. To determine if something adds value, it must be tied to an expectation. Most of the time, it needs to accomplish something that has been pre-determined and agreed upon – with your customer.

For your customer. Who is your customer? If could be your boss. It might be another department. And it could be an external entity that is willing to pay for a specific product or service. In any case, optimization bursts are always used to develop something that you have agreed to deliver to a specific customer.

We have three standard methodologies that we use for optimization bursts: Micro Bursts, Macro Bursts, and Process Optimizations Bursts – all using The DMAIC Way®.

What is The DMAIC Way®?

The DMAIC Way® (pronounced də-MAY-ick) is an acronym for Define, Measure, Analyze, Improve, and Control. The DMAIC Way® consists of nine steps that integrates Lean & Six Sigma that was introduced by organizations like Toyota, Motorola and General Electric. That sounds pretty complicated, but it's really just a thinking and problem-solving process.

The DMAIC Way®

- Focuses on nine specific questions.
- There are optimization tools that enable the user to think through these questions.
- The answers to these questions are displayed on an A3.

What's an A3? A3's were created by Toyota and it is a simple form – named after the size of the paper (~11"x17").

The DMAIC Way®
9-Step Process

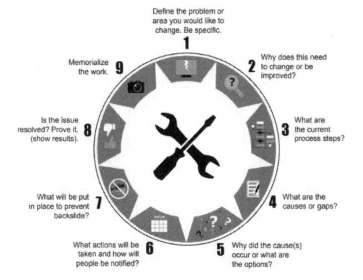

1 Define the problem or area you would like to change. Be specific.

2 Why does this need to change or be improved?

3 What are the current process steps?

4 What are the causes or gaps?

5 Why did the cause(s) occur or what are the options?

6 What actions will be taken and how will people be notified?

7 What will be put in place to prevent backslide?

8 Is the issue resolved? Prove it, (show results).

9 Memorialize the work.

The proven process to
Make it Better! Make it Stick!©

Micro Bursts™

Micro Bursts™ are a formal, week-long process that brings a cross-functional team (typically five to eight people) together to solve a problem. The team uses the 9-step DMAIC Way® model to deliver a solution for a customer. That customer could be organizational leaders, members of a specific department, or even an external customer.

Micro Bursts™ are facilitated by an Optimization Master Facilitator. And the cool thing is that it teaches novices how to solve problems AND use basic optimization tools WHILE they are delivering value for their customer!

Macro Bursts™

Macro Bursts are also formal in the sense that they are still facilitated by an Optimization Master Facilitator and participants still use the DMAIC Way® model. Macro Bursts™ teach individuals how to use intermediate optimization tools & lead a team WHILE they deliver a valuable solution for their customer.

Macro Bursts™ also provide individuals with an "optimization mindset" that allows them to contribute to and be an integral part of the leveling-up process. This foundation gives people throughout the organization the skills they need to find practical and sustainable methodologies to improve every-day work.

Process Optimization Bursts™

After individuals have been through a Micro Burst™ or a Macro Burst™, they are ready to work on their own. That's when Process Optimization Bursts™ come into play. They now have the skills and experiences they need to successfully set aside time that will accomplish something of value for their customer!

Now THAT's exciting!

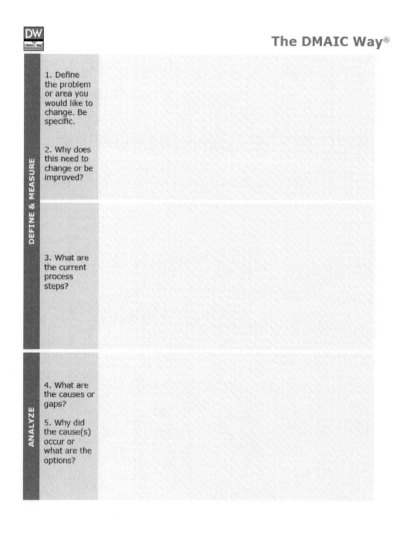

The DMAIC Way®

DEFINE & MEASURE

1. Define the problem or area you would like to change. Be specific.

2. Why does this need to change or be improved?

3. What are the current process steps?

ANALYZE

4. What are the causes or gaps?

5. Why did the cause(s) occur or what are the options?

A3 Storyboard

6. What actions will be taken and how will people be notified?

(Immediate and permanent fix, what else is impacted?)

7. What will be put in place to prevent backslide?

(What other processes/ systems are impacted, what metrics will be measured, what documents need updated, what training should be conducted/ created)

IMPROVE & CONTROL

8. Is the issue resolved? Prove it, (show results).

9. Memorialize the work by storing your A3.

OPTIMIZATION BURSTS
Reinforcement Resources

"I never learn anything talking. I only learn things when I ask questions."

– Lou Holtz

1. What issues or problems need to be solved at your organization?

2. If there was a good solution to the items in #1, why would it be beneficial to solve them?

3. Think about your team. How could you use the tools and level up their skills using The DMAIC Way®? Check out the templates: chiefoptimizationofficer.com/tools

11
MEASURE

"If you can't measure it, you can't improve it"

— unknown

We've worked with organizations that measure everything. They measure financial data. They measure sales. They measure productivity. They measure product quality. They measure safety. They measure the number of hours worked. They measure turnover. They measure employee satisfaction. They measure customer loyalty. We could go on and on...
Is all this data helpful? Useful? Do these organizations use the data they collect? More often than not, the answer is a resounding no! They spend time and money collecting it and yet they don't use most of it – which is a perfect example of wasted excellence! So, why measure at all?

Metrics, when done well, can:

- Drive improvements.
- Increase profitability, efficiency, and effectiveness.
- Determine what is and is not working.
- Verify that the organization is meeting their commitments.
- Focus resources on what is important.
- Communicate organizational priorities.

The problem is that too often, organizations don't measure well.

Let's look at one of our favorite movies, based on a book written by Michael Lewis, called Moneyball.[64] Moneyball showed how Billy Beane, then the General Manager of the Oakland Athletics baseball team, used metrics to build a winning baseball team.

Prior to 2002, the A's, like all baseball teams, used talent scouts to assess players. With traditional sports statistics in hand, talent scouts would go watch players in action on the field. Then they would use their personal baseball experience, intuition, and bias to determine if they thought highly enough of the player to add them to the roster.

This process resulted in a team of players that "looked" good. However, "looking good" was not a predictor of success.

In 2002 Billy, aided by Paul DePodesta, transformed the player acquisition process by identifying metrics that mattered. The old measure (batting average) was not a metric that mattered. A much better metric was a player's ability to get on base. The Oakland A's leveraged this superior metric in 2002 to identify the right players, spend half of what other teams spent on player salaries, and win 20 major league baseball games in a row – a feat that had not been accomplished in over 100 years!

A critical metric in baseball is a player's ability to get on base. What's yours?

We ask organizations six questions to help them identify what to measure.

- What does success look like?
- What 4-6 things have the biggest impact on our success?
- Over time, what outcome(s) correlate with success?
- Is the measurement driving the outcome you're looking for?
- Does the measure provide the information you need for decision making?
- Is the measure resulting in organizational behavior that you want and would be proud of?

What does success look like?

Alice in Wonderland, written by Lewis Carroll, contains some very interesting and profound truths, including: "If you don't know where you are going, any road will take you there."[65]

Do you know where your organization is going? Can you articulate what success looks like? Can you share it in the next 60 seconds? Most people can't. Heck, most people have trouble identifying and communicating their personal idea of success – let alone organizational success.

Unfortunately, if you can't name it, you can't measure it. Period.

In professional sports, defining success might seem pretty straightforward. Success = Winning. And maybe it's that uncomplicated for your organization.

- Success = profitability.
- Success = organizational sustainability.
- Success = market share percentage.
- Success = increased shareholder value.

For other organizations, it's not that obvious, so they buckle down and get their strategic planning done. And if they've done a good job, you'll see their definition of success embedded in their mission statements. Tesla is a great example. Their mission is "to accelerate the world's transition to sustainable energy."

Until you have identified and agreed upon what success looks like, you can measure all you want, but it will be an effort of wasted excellence. Without a clear destination, you simply won't know what metrics are truly important. Which means you won't have the "right" data to make data-based decisions.

What four-six things have the biggest impact on our success?

None of us likes to admit that we follow the crowd, but when it comes to metrics, many organizations do what everyone else is doing. The CHRO comes back from his HR Roundtable and wants to implement net promotor scores. Your CIO measures utilization because that's what his best friend's company is doing. Marketing is tracking costs per click and customer acquisition costs – well, because that's what the internet says to do. And of course, production is measuring throughput, first pass yield, raw materials demand, changeover time, machine downtime, and cycle time – because that's what all manufacturing companies do. I mean, haven't you read Deming?[66]

Getting metrics right is not about doing what everyone else is doing. It's about causation. Yes, your key metrics MAY match what others are doing. But don't get complacent. And don't just measure what's easy and comfortable. Dig deep. Do your homework. Focus on YOUR success criteria and look for cause and effect. Harvard Business Review says it this way:

"What you're after, then, are statistics that reliably reveal cause and effect. These have two defining characteristics: They are persistent, showing that the outcome of a given action at one time will be similar to the outcome of the same action at another time; and they are predictive—that is, there is a causal relationship between the action the statistic measures and the desired outcome."[67]

But here's the scary part. Most companies fail to link cause and effect, especially when they are looking at nonfinancial metrics.[68]

Over time, what outcome(s) correlate with success?

Even if an organization is trying to link cause and effect, we haven't met a company that got their metrics right the first time. You start with a best guess.

What are the four to six key things that you THINK will help you keep abreast of what is truly happening in the organization? You identify methodologies to gather the data. You build reports. You analyze the data. You tweak the data you are capturing. And then you rinse and repeat often, until you find cause and effect.

This process is not easy, nor does it happen overnight.

However, if an organization is patient and persistent, the result will be worthwhile data that:

- Drives the outcomes the organization is looking for.
- Helps the organization make better decisions.
- Results in organizational behaviors that they can be proud of.

If the organization is unwilling to do the work, they will have data, and best-case scenario – it won't be worth the time and effort it took to collect it. That's bad. But it could be worse.

Do the measures result in behaviors that you're proud of?

Do you remember the Wells Fargo scandal? Historically, Wells Fargo has been a highly respected organization. During the 2008 mortgage crisis, Wells became the third largest bank in the United States and Fortune Magazine suggested that Wells [avoided] "the rest of the industry's dumbest mistakes."[69] In early 2013, Fortune named Wells' Chairman and CEO "Banker of the Year."[70] In 2015, Wells Fargo was seventh on Barron's list of "Most Respected Companies."[71]

A year later, Wells was in trouble. Their employees had opened more than two million accounts without customer authorization. The result? Wells had to refund more than $2.6 million dollars to their customers. They paid a $185 million dollar settlement. And they ended up firing more than 5,300 employees.[72]

Unbelievable! What happened? Simply put – a metric drove an unintended organizational behavior.

We've all heard the phrase, "what gets measured gets done." An organization defines success, identifies four-six drivers of that success, finds methodologies to measure the drivers, and encourages employees to leverage and grow their skills and abilities to improve those drivers. And that is exactly what needs to happen. The goal is to tie the organization's definition of success with persistent and predictive measures that people can impact and control.

When the drivers of success are out of our control, it's a game of chance. Are we going to be lucky this time, or aren't we? Whether we like it or not, luck is a part of the equation. There is no sense, however, in measuring things that are random. So, measurements that matter need to be tied to drivers that can be impacted by employees and management.

The upside is that when people align with the measurement, you'll experience the success you were looking for. The downside is that people might "game" the system.

There may be some controversy over the Wells scandal. Some people may want to blame executive leadership. Others will point at the 5,300 employees who clearly did not follow policy. However, when you're concentrating on placing blame, you're looking in the wrong direction.

Anytime an organization puts a measure in place, there will be a reaction. The metric either will or will not measure and support the desired outcome. And it either will or will not result in organizational behaviors they will be proud of.

It's important that organizations recognize that metrics are not a once-and-done activity. Looking at one piece of the puzzle may provide you with a false positive. Think about it this way: if the CEO at Wells looked at the percentage of customers who added products in 2013, he might have believed – incorrectly – that the bank was increasing shareholder value.

Metrics need to be considered in context. Organizations need to:

- Recognize that what drives success today – may not drive success tomorrow.
- Continually evaluate how their metrics are driving managerial and employee behavior.
- Take time, every once in a while, to intentionally determine if the organization's metrics are still relevant.

Just like Michael J. Mauboussin said in his book, *The Success Equation*, "The drivers of value change over time, and so must your statistics."[73]

MEASURE
Reinforcement Resources
"One accurate measurement is worth a thousand expert opinions."
– Rear Admiral Grace M. Hopper

1. How would YOU answer our key measure questions? Key measures matrix: chiefoptimizationofficer.com/tools

2. What are you currently measuring? How do you use that information?

3. When was the last time you intentionally evaluated your metrics? What are you measuring that doesn't add value?

12
BRING PEOPLE ALONG

"Innovation comes only from readily and seamlessly sharing information rather than hoarding it."

— Tom Peters

Organizational Optimization doesn't happen just because you've hired a Chief Optimization Officer. One person, by themselves, cannot raise the organization's set point. It requires a tribe. It is the COptOs responsibility to bring the tribe along with them. And by now you know that it takes:

Success Skills
- Awareness
- Truth Telling
- Curiousness
- Gathering
- Ruthless Discernment
- Holistic Perspective

And Success Methodologies
- Facilitation
- Simplify
- Incremental Growth
- Optimizations Bursts
- Measure

To Bring People Along

Over the years, many organizations have brought us in to be their temporary COptO. It is a job we've come to relish. And when we work in this capacity, we typically have to manage and realize three things in order to bring people along:
- Assess Agreement
- Appraise the Organization Response to Optimization
- Execute the Sales Strategy

Assess Agreement

Assessing agreement is about ensuring we're on the same page. And even if heads are nodding in agreement and money has been put in the budget and consultants have been hired – it does not mean there is agreement.

Case in point...

A powerful statewide association contacted us about leveling up their leadership. After discussions with every member of the C-Suite, we moved forward with a plan that included 360-degree feedback, behavioral assessments, leadership workshops, and 1:1 executive coaching.

But a strange thing happened as we executed the

plan. We kept getting "yes, buts" from the CEO.

- "Yes, but you should have seen the mess it was before."
- "Yes, but it's not that bad."
- "Yes, but that's not the issue."
- "Yes, but what we're doing is good enough."

Of course, we had no one to blame but ourselves. We knew better, and we forgot to assess agreement BEFORE we got started. Assessing agreement is very simple and straightforward.

It's a matter of asking and discussing four very important questions:
- Do we agree that there is a problem (or that you have something you would like to optimize)?
- Do we have agreement on the problem (or the optimization)?

- Do we agree that it needs to be solved (or improved)?
- Do we agree on the solution?

If you cannot agree on the answers to these four questions, you will not bring people along.

Appraise the Organization's Response to Optimization

When we've been brought in to act as a temporary COptO, we often see three reactions to the organizational optimization process.

People in the organization are either:

- CAVE People
- Optimization Advocates
- The Movable Middle

Identifying who fits into what category and determining the best way to respond to these different perspectives is an important key if you want to bring people along.

CAVE People

You've met CAVE People before. They are the cousins to energy vampires, and they are known for being Constantly Against Virtually Everything. Most people distance themselves from CAVE People; however, if you want to bring people along, we recommend you give these cronies some consideration. Yes, CAVE People bring a lot of negativity into the equation, but there is a gift in there – somewhere.

Let's look at an example. Meet Juanita.

Juanita was the executive director of $3M nonprofit. When Juanita first joined the organization, there were 14 board members, one of whom was a CAVE person. We'll call her Lucy.

Lucy had this uncanny knack of finding fault with everything. If the organization was under budget, Juanita must not be providing enough services. If service numbers were up, Juanita must not be prioritizing. And if a new program was attracting a lot of attention, Lucy was concerned about the required resources.

Lucy's negativity never ended. And what's worse, Lucy always held her punches until the last minute. In board meeting after board meeting, the chair would open an agenda item, lead the discussion, narrow down the choices, and be ready for a motion – only to have Lucy throw a grenade into the mix right before the vote.

Sound familiar?

Some CAVE People are outwardly obvious. They share their negativity any chance they can. Some CAVE People are snipers like Lucy. They bide their time and strike at the last minute when there is not enough time left to refute them. And some CAVE People don't share their point of view publicly. They go underground.

The thing to remember is that people are simply trying to sell their point view. They might be selling by screaming and yelling, or by snatching victory out from under you at the last minute, or by stirring the pot behind your back. But those are just their sales tactics. And while you could try to fight fire with fire, we've found that the best way to handle CAVE People is to embrace the dissent and intentionally and purposefully give them a hearing.

You know that old joke about the kid who is asked why he is sooo happy about shoveling a pile of manure and replies by saying; "with this much shit, there's got to be a pony around here somewhere!" Yes, you may have to handle a ton of bull, AND if you listen carefully, CAVE People will point you to the pony – the gift.

> "The best way to handle CAVE People is to embrace the dissent and intentionally and purposefully give them a hearing."

Within CAVE People's rhetoric is a concern. And individuals other than CAVE People might share that same concern. So, when you give CAVE People a hearing you are learning what YOU need to know to sell YOUR point of view. In sales language, a concern is called an objection. And with advance notice of an objection, even a mediocre salesperson can come prepared with a solution. 😊

So how did Juanita solve her CAVE Person problem? She met with Lucy frequently and purposefully and intentionally asked Lucy to tell her what was wrong with specific ideas, presentations, potential solutions, etc. And then of course, Juanita asked Lucy how she would overcome these hurdles. Did that stop Lucy from being a CAVE Person? No. Did Lucy somehow become magically happy and satisfied? No.

What did change, however, is that Juanita stopped getting blindsided by a lack of knowledge. By listening to Lucy, Juanita was able to come to the table with a broader perspective and bring solutions that addressed the board's concerns.

You see, there is a pony in there somewhere.

Optimization Advocates

We admit it. We love Optimization Advocates. They are our people. They are risk-takers, energy-makers, and resistance-breakers. They are achievers who are naturally excited about new things. And to be honest, they optimize simply because that is what drives them. They are often dissatisfied or bored with the status quo and are constantly on the lookout for what's next and what's possible.

It's easy to spot an Optimization Advocate. They:

- Don't require a lot of data and information before they make a decision.
- Adopt new technology – when it first comes out.
- Say: "Heck – let's try it!"
- Are unfazed if something doesn't work perfectly.
- Pivot quickly and easily.

When you're in the business of raising an organization's set point, Optimization Advocates are your go-to people. Because they are undaunted by the prospect of failure, they'll try things out for you, provide you with feedback, give you suggestions to make it better, and then try it out again after you've made some tweaks. Even more exciting – throughout the entire process, they'll sing your praises, because they enjoy going on a "what-if," "what's next," and "what's possible" journey with someone they consider a peer.

So, what does it take to get an Optimization Advocate on your side? Simply ask them to play – early in the process! Then give them an important job to do. You don't want your Optimization Advocates to get bored. When they get bored, they will move on to another opportunity.

The Moveable Middle

Okay, here's an oldie but a goodie. In 1962, E.M. Rogers developed the Diffusion of Innovation (DOI) Theory. The theory suggested that new ideas are embraced over time based on a standard bell curve. About 16% of the population adopts an idea quickly. Another 16% come to the table a little late. And the majority – around 68% of the population – falls somewhere in the middle.[74]

That 68% is what we call the Moveable Middle.

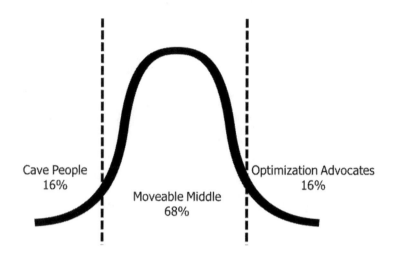

Cave People
16%

Optimization Advocates
16%

Moveable Middle
68%

The Moveable Middle is often ignored. Optimization Advocates get a lot of time and attention because they easily plug into and support leveling up – which makes them a joy to be around.

CAVE People get a lot of time and attention because they're stirring the pot. And we often spend too much time trying to shut down all of their drama. So with our attention pointed elsewhere, we often don't MAKE time for the Moveable Middle. And that is a mistake! Imagine organizational optimization as a tug of war game. On one side you have your Optimization Advocates. They are pulling with all their might trying to convince the organization that THEIR way is the way to go. On the other side of the rope, you have your CAVE People. They are pulling with all their might trying to convince the organization that THEIR way is the way to go. And according to E.M. Rogers – it's a stalemate. Neither side is making make enough headway to win.

That's because both sides are ignoring the Moveable Middle.

In Malcolm Gladwell's book, called The Tipping Point, he wrote, "Look at the world around you. It may seem like an immovable, implacable place. It is not. With the slightest push — in just the right place — it can be tipped."[75] And based upon Gladwell's Law of the Few and the scientists at Rensselaer Polytechnic Institute, it only takes another 10% before the majority adopts an idea. That 10% can be found in the Moveable Middle.[76] And that's REALLY good news.

Trying to bring 68% of the people along with you on your optimization journey would be an impossible task. But 10%? That's doable. And it may be easier that you think.

If you've invited Optimization Advocates into the fold early in the process and have involved them in the work, their enthusiasm will spread.

If you've taken the time to listen to your CAVE People and have looked for the pony, you will have already identified and addressed many of the organization's concerns.

And, if you've successfully addressed the concerns of one CAVE Person and recruited them to your point of view, you will have added a very powerful backer. A CAVE Person who becomes a supporter has the ability to persuade other CAVE People. Afterall, they have mean sales skills.

Execute the Sales Strategy

Sales is not a dirty word. We all sell things. We convince our kids to eat vegetables. We persuade our spouse to go out to dinner. We encourage our neighbors to keep their dog out of our yard. And we coax our boss to extend a deadline. Each one of these endeavors requires a sales strategy. We've found, however, that the selling is not the key, nor is the strategy itself – it's the execution that's important. And how we go about the process actually makes all the difference in the world.

Point one: Over-Communicate

The more times people see or hear something, the more they remember it, and the more normal it becomes. The more normal it becomes, the more they trust it. What's the magic number of times that a message needs to be repeated? Seven. SEVEN. Seven Times. SEVEN TIMES. Did we say seven? Seven Times? Yes, it really takes seven times!

This is not new information. And in some ways, we can't believe we still need to talk about this. The sad fact is that many organizations don't put this idea into practice. And six months later they can't understand why their staff doesn't get it. Ummm...oh yeah, we didn't over-communicate. $hit!!

Point two: Listen.

No plan is perfect. Remember, your people are brilliant if you allow them to be. So, listen. Listen to what is being said. Listen to what is not being said. Pay attention. Ask questions. Look for dissent.

There is information to collect and lessons to be learned during execution.   So, MAKE the time to connect with people and see how they are being impacted.

Point three: Adjust.

Your plan is not the Ten Commandments. It was not decreed from above. Nor is it chiseled in stone. It's just a plan. And it can be modified, refined, and even improved! 😄

So, when you listen, look for what's right about other people's perspectives, then adjust as you go. If you want to bring people along you will need to listen and take action on their ideas and suggestions. Otherwise, you'll be all alone on that mountain top.

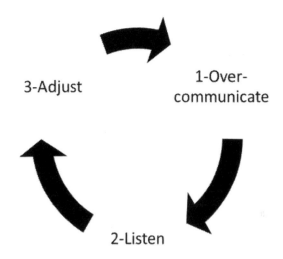

3-Adjust

1-Over-
communicate

2-Listen

One last lesson:

Choose your communication methodologies carefully. How you share your message should be predicated on your relationship with that individual.

For your best relationships, you can use a text or an email. Why? When you have strong relationships with individuals, you trust one another. You give one another the benefit of the doubt. You don't have to be worried about the words you use or the "tone" of your message. You understand one another. And IF the message came off "wrong," they would follow up with you and ask for clarification before jumping to conclusions.

For your good, but not intimate, relationships, pick up the phone. A phone call will give you the opportunity to gauge the other individual's reactions, respond to their questions, and ensure mutual understanding. More and more people are taking the lazy way out and relying on texts and emails. Don't fall into this trap. There is an art to a successful phone call. Make sure you keep and/or build this skill.

Finally, for new or strained relationships, you need to be face-to-face.

Building and repairing relationships requires a deeper level of intimacy and vulnerability. Science suggests that you need to be within four feet of an individual if you're going to build intimacy – even professional intimacy.[78] Of course, there are times – like in the midst of a global pandemic – that it is not wise or possible to be face-to-face. When that's the case, learning to create intimacy virtually becomes extremely beneficial.

Chief Optimization Officer

BRING PEOPLE ALONG
Reinforcement Resources

"Alone we can do so little; together we can do so much."

– Helen Keller

1. Think about a situation where it would be important to Access Agreement.

   - Do we agree that there is a problem (or that you have something you would like to optimize)?
   - Do we have agreement on the problem (or the optimization)?
   - Do we agree that it needs to be solved (or improved)?
   - Do we agree on the solution?

2. Identify your CAVE People and go look for the pony.

3. Who are your Optimization Advocates? How are you involving them?

4. How are you executing your sales strategy?

PART III
CONCLUSION & RESOURCES

13
CONCLUSION

"And now....the rest of the story... "

– Paul Harvey

We've made the case that a successful Chief Optimization Officer is a rare talent. They have an extremely high level of awareness. They are truth tellers who are curious. They are constantly gathering people and information. They know when to say no. And they see the big picture.

We've also provided you with tactics that a COptO can use to maximize their efforts including facilitation, simplification, incremental growth, optimization bursts and measuring well.

The REAL question however, is does this role work? Can it really make a difference?

Let us introduce you to Andrea.

Andrea works for a large, multi-national company. Believe it or not – she's come up through the ranks and has worked – at the same location – for almost 14 years.

Much like Paul, who we introduced you to in Chapter 1, Andrea started her career as a Quality Engineer. Andrea however was promoted three times and ended up leading the Quality department within six years of joining the organization. During that time, Andrea built a reputation for asking good questions, truly listening, and bringing people together to solve problems.

For example – like most organizations – there was a lot of finger-pointing going on at Andrea's company. The data would highlight a problem and each of the departments would quickly lay the blame at the feet of another department – basically saying – it's not me – it's them. That tactic constantly stalled progress. Andrea got sick and tired of it – and she decided to do something about it.

So, when the organization was facing a major re-work issue – Andrea pulled a cross-functional team together and facilitated what we now call a Macro Burst™ workshop. In less than a week this cross-functional frontline team identified the root cause of the issue, considered options and alternatives, identified the solution that had the greatest impact, tested it to ensure that it would consistently deliver the quality they were looking for and presented the recommended solution – along with the supporting data – to their superiors.

Oh, if you could have been there to see the look on their bosses faces. It was priceless!

The result? Their recommended solution reduced product non-conformities and rework by 15% and resulted in a $16M savings in the first year that it was implemented. Maybe even more importantly – the department managers stopped pointing figures and started concentrating on problem solving.

Andrea was beginning to gather people and bring them along!

Very soon after that big win the organization promoted Andrea to head the "new" Standardization department. Andrea continued to hone her skills during this three-year stint.

One of her important learning lessons came when the plant manager asked her to take on a pet project – which really meant pushing his agenda through the organization.

That was an epic fail. This was what taught Andrea her first discernment lesson. When the "solution" has already been pre-determined by management – just say no thank you!

Andrea learned another lesson when the organization wanted to set a goal to accumulate black belts. Somehow the organization had gotten fixated on the wrong metric. The number of black belts in an organization is not a predictor of success.

These growing pains were very good spotlight moments in Andrea's career. Without them, she might be making the same mistakes today. Andrea, however, learned from these situations and continued to grow and level up.

So, if these were Andrea's missteps, what were her successes during this time-period? Well, even if the number of black belts is not the right metric – you can leverage black belt expertise. Andrea worked with her internal black belts – and frontline staff – to reduce organizational complexity. That project increased plant productivity by 15%! Can you say drop the mic? And of course, that resulted in Andrea's next promotion. The organization invited her to be the Director of Continuous Improvement (CI).

Andrea held this position for just under 4 years. During that time, she:

- Deployed a single CI framework that focused on business goals and customer savings that achieved over $250M in annual savings.

- Established an enterprise-wide Learning Management System and Corporate University, which increased learning by 35% and reduced the time to job qualification by 54%.

- Enabled the organization to achieve national recognition with Baldrige.

Even with all of that, one of our favorite experiences during this time was when we had the opportunity to join a plant tour that Andrea was leading for a group of C-Suite corporate executives. As you might expect, when "corporate" is visiting there's a lot of spit and polish involved – so the plant was in tip-top shape. And of course, the staff was prepped. At each stop on the journey one team member was given the responsibility to explain what they did in the department and how their work contributed to the success of the organization.

Everything was going well – until the tour group got to their fourth destination on the tour. Then a curious executive, with a very stern demeanor, asked about "all the documents plastered on the walls." Immediately, we were concerned. This was off script. We hadn't talked about it. We didn't know if Andrea had prepped the team for this question. And all we heard was condemnation.

Andrea calmly called on a front line employee to explain what it was. To this day we do not know what that frontline employee was thinking AND he was brilliant. He walked over to the wall. Pulled down an A3 that his team had completed the previous week and explained the 9 questions – perfectly – to this group of suits.

The exec's follow-up question was priceless. "Where did you learn to do that?" The simple answer: "Everyone here goes through The DMAIC Way® workshops. It's how we make things better."

We could not have paid someone to give a better answer. And what still brings us joy today – is that he was telling the truth. Andrea was not a lone wolf CI guru. In just a few years, she had successfully infected the entire organization. The plant and the people that worked there were no longer satisfied with just doing their job. They were not happy with simply perpetuating the status quo. They truly wanted to make things better. They wanted to level up. They wanted to identify ways to optimize their contributions and enable the organization to be more and do more. And they did it. On a daily basis.

Where is Andrea now? Isn't it obvious? She's in the C-Suite!.

14
CHIEF OPTIMIZATION OFFICER JOB DESCRIPTION

We promised to provide you the world's first Chief Optimization Officer job description. Assembling the best skills, abilities, and our manifesto, this job description provides you a guide to identify and either grow or hire your own Chief Optimization Officer.

The Chief Optimization Officer (COptO) creates unique value by anticipating and executing to the evolving needs of the customer, product, and services, and connects actions to align these needs to achieve organizational goals in the most effective and efficient way possible.

The successful COptO drives incremental growth through the obsession of aligning and optimizing all factors of the organization – supply chain, talent, operations, finance, sales -- to have consistent and predictable execution each day while enabling ripple-free growth.

The COptO, will lead a team with the purpose of optimizing the entire organization. This team works as the Optimization Gurus and program managers to identify opportunities and work across functional teams to align end-to-end processes, ensure effective processes and sustainable process outcomes. The COptO will own the multi-year prioritized optimization roadmap supporting growth and business objectives.

Base Responsibilities

- Use data driven analytics to work across teams to ensure agreement of a prioritized roadmap to ruthlessly discern tradeoff decisions and / or leverage metrics to track success measures and ROI.
- In alignment with the Senior Leadership Team, support the organization to successfully identify, document, improve, and adopt improvement.
- Continuously evolve and improve the impact of the optimization efforts.
- Engage leaders and team members in the growth and optimization process.
- Build awareness for yourself, Optimization Gurus, and the entire organization to increase everyone's Awareness Quotient.
- See the organization holistically, understanding that the sum of the parts must work together to be optimized.
- Be bold in truth telling to challenge the Senior Leadership Team and organization alike of options, alternatives, innovation, potential risks, and actions necessary for optimization.
- Gather information and data to provide thought leadership for industry best practices and approach to build an Optimization Culture.

Communication and Relationship Management

- Identify opportunities for new projects that will positively impact the organization.
- Create strong business partnerships with all levels of the organization and build Centers of Excellence to integrate strategic business initiatives, planning projections, and performance improvement into the overall long-range optimization roadmap.
- Present information clearly and understand organizational context and nuances.
- Identify appropriate tools and templates to use for Optimization Bursts.
- Produce consumable communication and deliverables.

Optimization Roadmap Oversight

- Take initiative to ensure success of the optimization roadmap.
- Set the example and provide strategic oversight and direction in a professional manner with a personal style.
- Identify and track key metrics that help understand the progress of the roadmap.
- Gather necessary information, customer needs, stakeholder requirements, etc. to ensure the continued evolution of the optimization roadmap.
- Collaborate with organization to ensure alignment/changes to the optimization roadmap, playbook, communication, training, and/or optimization activities are identified and in place to successfully deliver solutions.
- Guide business through information and data to ensure meaningful insights are extracted and can be used to produce data-driven decisions and business outcomes.

Required Qualifications

- 10+ years experience in Organizational Development, Continuous Improvement, Operations, or similar.
- 5+ years leading teams through process optimization and/or change management.
- Experience with thinking strategically and executing tactically.
- Advanced conceptual, analytical, and problem-solving abilities.
- Experience leading complex cross-functional projects, with proven ability to meet challenging organizational objectives.
- Experience partnering at all levels of the organization to design and implement programs and solutions.
- Proven ability to use good business judgment, exceptional communication skills, and diplomatic conflict resolution.
- Ability to effectively participate on cross-functional teams with a consulting style to meet established goals and objectives.
- Possess problem-solving ability, leadership skills and the ability to foster interpersonal relationships.

Preferred Qualifications
- Experience with DMAIC, Six Sigma, Lean, and/or Total Quality Management process optimizations.
- BS, MS or higher degree in Operations Management, I/O Psychology, Industrial Engineering/Technology, Quality Management, Organizational Development desired.

Optimized Skills & Certifications
- Certified Master Facilitator.
- Certified The DMAIC Way® Master Black Belt.
- Certified Talent Optimization Consultant.

Download a copy of the Job Description at chiefoptimizationofficer.com/tools

REFERENCES

1) Wikipedia:
https://en.wikipedia.org/wiki/Compaq_Portable#cite_note-oldcomputers-11
2) Sosik, J. J. (2001). Self-other agreement on charismatic leadership: Relationships with work attitudes and managerial performance. *Group & Organization Management, 26*(4), 484-511.
3) Berson, Y., & Sosik, J. J. (2007). The relationship between self—other rating agreement and influence tactics and organizational processes. Group & Organization Management, 32(6), 675-698.
4) Sosik, J. J., & Megerian, L. E. (1999). Understanding Leader Emotional Intelligence and Performance: The Role of Self-Other Agreement on Transformational Leadership Perceptions. Group & Organization Management, 24(3), 367–390. Sosik, 2001
5) Eurich, T. (2017). Insight: The power of self-awareness in a self-deluded world. Macmillan.
6) Cherniss, C., & Goleman, D. (2001). The emotionally intelligent workplace: How to select for, measure, and improve emotional intelligence in individuals, groups, and organizations.
7) Ostroff, C., Atwater, L. E., & Feinberg, B. J. (2004). Understanding self-other agreement: A look at rater and ratee characteristics, context, and outcomes. Personnel Psychology, 57(2), 333-375.
8) Drigas, A. S., & Papoutsi, C. (2018). A new layered model on emotional intelligence. *Behavioral Sciences, 8*(5), 45.
9) Elias, A. A., & Cavana, R. Y. (2000, December). Stakeholder analysis for systems thinking and modeling. In *Victoria University of Wellington, New Zealand. Conference paper.*

10) Khalsa, M., & Illig, R. (2008). *Let's Get Real Or Let's Not Play: Transforming the Buyer/seller Relationship*. Penguin.
11) Covey, S. R. (2013). *The 7 habits of highly effective people: Powerful lessons in personal change*. Simon and Schuster.
12) Goleman, D. (2017). *Leadership that gets results (Harvard business review classics)*. Harvard Business Press.
13) Battilana, J., & Casciaro, T. (2013). The network secrets of great change agents. *Harvard Business Review, 91*(7), 62-68.
14) Maister, D. H., Galford, R., & Green, C. (2021). *The trusted advisor*. Free Press.
15) O'Connor, Peg. May 2014. Why is it so hard to trust ourselves? Psychology Today. https://www.psychologytoday.com/us/blog/philosophy-stirred-not-shaken/201405/why-is-it-so-hard-trust-yourself
16) Maister, D. H., Galford, R., & Green, C. (2021). *The trusted advisor*. Free Press.
17) Burg, B., & Mann, J. D. (2007). The Go-Giver. *New York: Portfolio*.
18) Arbinger Institute. (2010). *Leadership and self-deception: Getting out of the box*. Berrett-Koehler Publishers.
19) Gino, F. (2018). Why curiosity matters?. *Harvard Business Review, September-October issue*, 47-61.
20) Gino, Francesca. "The business case for curiosity." *Harvard Business Review* 96, no. 5 (2018): 48-57.
21) MIT Policies & Procedures: https://policies.mit.edu/policies-procedures/20-faculty-and-other-academic-appointments/22-special-professorial-appointments

22) Gino, Francesca. "The business case for curiosity." *Harvard Business Review* 96, no. 5 (2018): 48-57.

23) Gino, Francesca. "The business case for curiosity." *Harvard Business Review* 96, no. 5 (2018): 48-57.

24) Catmull, E. (2008). *How Pixar fosters collective creativity*. Boston, MA: Harvard Business School Publishing.

25) Galef, J. (2021). *The Scout Mindset: Why Some People See Things Clearly and Others Don't*. Penguin.

26) Galef, J. (2021). *The Scout Mindset: Why Some People See Things Clearly and Others Don't*. Penguin.

27) Gino, Francesca. "The business case for curiosity." *Harvard Business Review* 96, no. 5 (2018): 48-57.

28) The Hunt: https://www.survivalinternational.org/galleries/hunters

29) Kaplan, D. (2000). The darker side of the" original affluent society". *Journal of Anthropological Research*, *56*(3), 301-324.

30) Laal, M., & Ghodsi, S. M. (2012). Benefits of collaborative learning. *Procedia-social and behavioral sciences*, *31*, 486-490.

31) Carroll, L. (2001). *Alice in wonderland and through the looking glass*. Bloomsbury Publishing.

32) Rice, K. Bleacher Report. 2009. Golf Strategy: Play Your Game Backwards for lower scores. https://bleacherreport.com/articles/168843-play-your-game-backwards-for-lower-scores

33) NIST. 2021-2022 Edition, Baldrige Excellence Framework, https://www.nist.gov/baldrige/publications/baldrige-excellence-framework/businessnonprofit

34) Hunt, V., Prince, S., Dixon-Fyle, S., & Dolan, K. (2020). *Diversity wins*. McKinsey.

35) Bourke, J., & Dillon, B. (2018). The diversity and inclusion revolution: Eight powerful truths. *Deloitte Review, 22*, 82-95.
36) Reynolds, A., & Lewis, D. (2017). Teams solve problems faster when they're more cognitively diverse. *Harvard Business Review, 30*.
37) People Management. 2017. Diversity drives better decisions. https://web.archive.org/web/20201120163033/https:/www.peoplemanagement.co.uk/experts/research/diversity-drives-better-decisions

38) KIMT3. 2018. Construction Error Delaying Exit Ramp on I-35 at Ames. https://www.kimt.com/content/news/Construction-error-delaying-new-exit-ramp-on-I-35-at-Ames-488014681.html
39) Tost, L. P., Gino, F., & Larrick, R. P. (2013). When power makes others speechless: The negative impact of leader power on team performance. *Academy of Management Journal, 56*(5), 1465-1486.
40) Tost, L. P., Gino, F., & Larrick, R. P. (2013). When power makes others speechless: The negative impact of leader power on team performance. *Academy of Management Journal, 56*(5), 1465-1486.
41) Clark, T. R. (2020). *The 4 stages of psychological safety: Defining the path to inclusion and innovation.* Berrett-Koehler Publishers.
42) Inc. Tusk, B. (2017). Want to Succeed? Try Impatience. https://www.inc.com/bradley-tusk/want-to-succeed-try-impatience.html
43) Act, A. (1970). Occupational safety and health act of 1970. *Public Law, 91,* 596.
44) Comaford-Lynch, C. (2013). *Smart Tribes: How teams become brilliant together.* Portfolio.
45) Zani, M. (2021). The Science of Dream Teams: How Talent Optimization Can Drive Engagement, Productivity, and Happiness. McGraw-Hill.

46) Kermisch, R & Fallis, J. (2017). Killing Complexity Before Complexity Kills Growth. https://www.bain.com/insights/killing-complexity-before-complexity-kills-growth/. Bain.

47) Whitehead, N. (2014, July). People would rather be electrically shocked than left alone with their thoughts. In *American Association for the Advancement of Science*.

48) Ward, D., Barakat, S., Cockburn, C., & Ellis, S. (2014). FIRE. *How Fast, Inexpensive, Restrained, and Elegant Methods Ignite Innovation. Harper Business*.

49) James Weldon Johnson, Wikipedia. https://en.wikipedia.org/wiki/Dem_Bones

50) Reis, E. (2011). The lean startup. *New York: Crown Business, 27*.

51) Parkinson, C. N. (1960). Parkinson's Laws. *SDL Rev., 5*, 1.

52) Ward, D. (2015). *The Simplicity Cycle: A Field Guide to Making Things Better Without Making Them Worse*. HarperCollins.

53) Raymond, E. (1999). The cathedral and the bazaar. *Knowledge, Technology & Policy, 12*(3), 23-49.

54) DePillis, L & Sherman, I. CNN. (2018). https://www.cnn.com/interactive/2018/10/business/amazon-history-timeline/index.html

55) Entrepreneur. (2021). Apply Incremental Innovation to Cope With the Crisis. https://www.entrepreneur.com/article/364711

56) Noble, C. (2011). *Clay Christensen's milkshake marketing*. Harvard Business School Working Knowledge.

57) Cecere, L. (2013). New products: More costly and more important. *URL https://www. forbes. com/sites/loracecere/2013/12/11/new-products-more-costly-and-more-important*.

58) Shapo, A. (2020). How Customer Feedback Surveys Help Apple Maintains Industry Leadership. https://www.myfeelback.com/en/blog/how-customer-feedback-surveys-helps-apple-maintains-industry-leadership
59) ACSI. (2021), https://www.theacsi.org/
60) Mahipal, A. (2021). Report: Brand loyalty at an all-time high of 92% for Apple as Android brands take a dive. https://www.sellcell.com/blog/cell-phone-brand-loyalty-2021/
61) Bernazzani, S. (2021). Here's Why Customer Retention is So Important for ROI, Customer Loyalty, and Growth. https://blog.hubspot.com/service/customer-retention
62) Lincoln. (2012). https://www.rottentomatoes.com/m/lincoln_2011/quotes/
63) Quora, Inc., (2018). Jeff Bezos Uses This Strategy to Make Better, Faster Decisions. https://www.inc.com/quora/jeff-bezos-uses-this-strategy-to-make-better-faster-decisions.html
64) Lewis, M. (2004). *Moneyball: The art of winning an unfair game*. WW Norton & Company.
65) Carroll, L. (2001). *Alice in wonderland and through the looking glass*. Bloomsbury Publishing.
66) Deming, W. E., & Edwards, D. W. (1982). *Quality, productivity, and competitive position* (Vol. 183). Cambridge, MA: Massachusetts Institute of Technology, Center for advanced engineering study.
67) Mauboussin, M. J. (2012). The true measures of success. *Harvard Business Review, 90*(10), 46-56.
68) Ittner, C. D., & Larcker, D. F. (2003). Coming up short on nonfinancial performance measurement. *Harvard business review, 81*(11), 88-95.
69) Sullivan, J. Fortune. (2012). Riders on the storm. https://fortune.com/2012/11/21/riders-on-the-storm/

70) Aspan, M. (2013). Wells Fargo's John Stumpf, the 2013 Banker of the Year'. *American Banker.*
71) Baron's Ranking. (2015). https://www.rankingthebrands.com/The-Brand-Rankings.aspx?rankingID=307&year=951
72) Tayan, B. (2019). The Wells Fargo cross-selling scandal. *Rock Center for Corporate Governance at Stanford University Closer Look Series: Topics, Issues and Controversies in Corporate Governance No. CGRP-62 Version, 2,* 17-1.
73) Mauboussin, M. J. (2012). *The success equation: Untangling skill and luck in business, sports, and investing.* Harvard Business Review Press.

74) Miller, R. L. (2015). Rogers' innovation diffusion theory (1962, 1995). In *Information seeking behavior and technology adoption: Theories and trends* (pp. 261-274). IGI Global.

75) Gladwell, M. (2006). *The tipping point: How little things can make a big difference*. Little, Brown.

76) DeMarco, G. (2011). Minority Rules: Scientists Discover Tipping Point for the Spread of Ideas. Rensselaer Polytechnic Institute (RPI).

77) Assemblo. (2017). Repetition is key: why frequency makes your marketing effective. https://assemblo.com/blog/repetition-is-key-why-frequency-makes-your-marketing-effective/

78) Haddad, A., Doherty, R., & Purtilo, R. (2019). Respectful communication in an information age. *Health Professional and Patient Interaction*, 141-165.

ABOUT THE AUTHORS

Scott Burgmeyer is the Founder & CEO of Creative Solutions Group. For more than 30 years he has worked and consulted in virtually all industries, including manufacturing, technology, education, and health care. He held roles such as QA Manager, CI Manager, Organizational Development, Human Resources, SVP Quality & Improvement, and Chief Improvement Officer.

Scott is a lifelong learner, professor, speaker and author of multiple books, articles and journal publications. As a Master Black Belt and creator of The DMAIC Way®, his goal is for everyone to Make it Better! Make it Stick!

Tammy K Rogers began her career at a startup company in Minneapolis designing employee satisfaction surveys. Within six months she was tapped to lead the new training and development division.

Tammera has written more than 50 internationally distributed training programs and worked with best-selling authors like James Autry and Bob Nelson. In 1995 Tammera ventured out on her own, founding three organizations, and today is leading her company, Aveea Partners. Tammera is best known for advising leaders and organizations to become more thorough and develop new ways of thinking, attitudes and behaviors that transfer to the real world results.

Made in the USA
Middletown, DE
24 May 2022

66157740R00142